CHASING TONE

HOW ROB TURNER AND EMG REVOLUTIONIZED THE GUITAR'S SOUND

Jim Reilly

ROWMAN & LITTLEFIELD
Lanham • Boulder • New York • London

Published by Rowman & Littlefield
An imprint of The Rowman & Littlefield Publishing Group, Inc.
4501 Forbes Boulevard, Suite 200, Lanham, Maryland 20706
www.rowman.com

86-90 Paul Street, London EC2A 4NE

British Library Cataloguing in Publication Information Available

Library of Congress Cataloging-in-Publication Data

Names: Reilly, Jim, 1968– author.
Title: Chasing tone : how Rob Turner and EMG revolutionized the guitar's
    sound / Jim Reilly.
Description: Lanham : Rowman & Littlefield Publishers, 2023. | Includes
    bibliographical references and index.
Identifiers: LCCN 2023003352 (print) | LCCN 2023003353 (ebook) | ISBN
    9781538181737 (cloth) | ISBN 9781538181744 (ebook)
Subjects: LCSH: Turner, Rob, 1953– | EMG, Inc.—Biography. | Electric
    guitar. | Bass guitar. | Guitar—Electronic equipment. | Bass
    guitar—Electronic equipment. | LCGFT: Biographies.
Classification: LCC ML424.T87 R45 2023 (print) | LCC ML424.T87 (ebook) |
    DDC 787.87/19092 [B]—dc23/eng/20230209
LC record available at https://lccn.loc.gov/2023003352
LC ebook record available at https://lccn.loc.gov/2023003353

*This book is dedicated to fathers and families
and the joy of creating together.*

He who works with his hands is a laborer.
He who works with his hands and his head is a craftsman.
He who works with his hands and his head and his heart is
an artist.

—Saint Francis of Assisi

I saved your ass!!! Get to work!

—Sonoma County public defender
Gene Tunney's directive to Rob Turner, 1973

CONTENTS

FOREWORD

Rob Turner and his company, EMG, are a success story on many levels. In its nearly half century of operation, the company has become one of the most important guitar pickup manufacturers on the planet. Founded on innovation, bold ideas, hard work, and inventiveness, EMG came about as a result of one monumental invention: a guitar pickup with a preamplifier built in.

Virtually all successful inventions have these things in common: novelty, ingenuity, and utility. Like a three-legged stool, though, if one of these three attributes is missing, the odds against acceptance, let alone a long life in the marketplace, are incredibly slim. If something is merely novel, like the legendary Pet Rock or the hula hoop, it can be a shooting star—flying high, selling fast, and then burning out. Cleverness (a.k.a. ingenuity) can provide some initial mileage for a product, but it's often based on curiosity on the part of potential customers. The two-wheel, stand-up-to-drive Segway with its long, cagey lead-up to its initial unveiling and then its quick petering out in the marketplace is a case in point. If an item is purely utilitarian, it may be accepted but may not ever be much of a star in the wider marketplace (think of those little needle threaders or the valve caps on inflatable tires—very useful, but not the basis of legends nor of legendary sales).

We take many successful inventions for granted probably because they were so successful that they became ubiquitous. In addition, many have been around so long that we don't give a thought to a world before they existed or, in fact, that so many things surrounding us were ever considered inventions at all. There was a world before television and microwave ovens, and there were once cars without airbags or seatbelts. Someone invented the telephone, the photocopier, computers, the laser printer, the zipper, the lightbulb, nylon, and so forth, not to mention the whole idea of printing and widely distributing books. We don't think of them as inventions, but at one time, they were presented as such, and they were major achievements.

All of these are examples of combinations of that which is novel, ingenious, and useful, solving problems that people were keenly aware of or delivering solutions to problems that people didn't know existed. The best and longest-lived usually boast one more element, the very reason they have staying power: a receptive world. Years ago, I used to research guitar history by poring over the stacks of printed patents at the US Patent & Trademark Office's clearing house in Sunnyvale, California. It was a treasure trove of ideas that were registered for protection against those who might try to duplicate them. Judging by the sheer number of patents, I can assure you there have been far more inventions than successful products—by a long shot. Almost all were novel. Some were utterly ingenious. Others were useful, or they would have been, had they ever reached the marketplace.

This brings to mind another factor in an invention's success: delivering not just a product but an ecosystem. In 2001 Apple introduced the wildly successful iPod music player into a market already full of other good MP3-format music players. But what was Apple's greatest idea at the time? They introduced not just the iPod but also the Apple Store and iTunes, a place to purchase music and a means of organizing and managing it, respectively. This combination proved to be a colossally successful ecosystem, something nobody else making MP3 players or peddling online music offered.

So where does the concept of an ecosystem collide with Rob Turner, EMG, and guitar and bass pickups? The electric guitar is a perfect example of an ecosystem (albeit smaller than Apple's) that had to be created, even if nobody realized it initially. After all, what good is an amplifier without a guitar or bass to plug into it? And what good is an electric guitar or bass if it doesn't have an amp to translate its sound into something that can be heard in a venue larger than an easy chair? It wasn't until about a century ago that the notion of amplifying a guitar was tried. During a time when Gibson only made acoustic guitars, mandolins, and banjos, Lloyd Loar, who was an acoustician and engineer there, experimented with magnetic pickups on various stringed instruments. The amplifier already existed, and the pickups he employed were magnets with coils of wire wrapped around them, similar to what you'd find in a telephone of the day to translate a person's voice into electrical signals that would run through wire and cables and be turned into sound by the telephone at the other end.

By the time Rob started a business creating pickups with preamps inside, the nascent market for replacement parts—including pickups—was about to explode. Readers of the only major guitar-related magazine at the time, *Guitar Player*, began seeing small ads in its issues for replacement pickups or pickup modification by previously nonexistent companies. Nearly a half century later, some of them are now heavyweights in the music industry, providing thousands and thousands of replacement pickups to do-it-yourselfers and guitar technicians, as well as supplying pickups to major guitar manufacturers. At that time, however, these companies typically consisted of one or two people with soldering irons and voltmeters, working out of repair shops, usually occupying much of their time fixing and adjusting.

I started working as an assistant editor at *Guitar Player* magazine in June 1977, then worked my way up to managing editor and remained there until 1991, specializing in following the technologies that were coming fast and furious during one of the golden eras for guitar and bass. One attribute was apparent in most guitarists, though: One part of them wanted to create a sound that nobody else had heard before, but the other part was very conservative regarding what a guitar consisted of and looked like. And they were very wary of modifications to their instruments. And although a spate of new signal modifiers such as the wah-wah pedal, the fuzz box (distortion), and the phase shifter could be added in the signal path between guitar and amp to tweak the sound, it was the rare guitarist who would accept having their beloved instrument altered in any visible way. So unless an aftermarket pickup directly fit the same size and shape of the original, many guitarists weren't interested.

While most of the aftermarket pickups offered then were created primarily to provide a "hotter" signal to produce more distortion through an amplifier, Rob Turner's were more sophisticated. By employing different magnets and coil-winding techniques and by placing the preamp right inside the pickup, he found a way to not only duplicate the physical dimensions of the original pickups but also to remove spurious noise that plagued virtually all single-coil pickups (the most famous being on Fender Stratocaster guitars). Could it be a cleaner, stronger signal without noise, even near fluorescent light fixtures or the whirring blenders operating in the ever-present bar at so many clubs? Yes, and that's a combination of attributes worth pursuing.

When it came to accommodating the dual mindset of guitarists who wanted a better sound but didn't want to deface their instruments, EMG pickups had a huge leg up: The "secret sauce" of their noise-killing preamp was that it took up no extra room inside a guitar because it was in the pickup itself. They looked like regular, stock pickups, so they didn't mess with an instrument's visual personality. Rob Turner had created an ecosystem, a self-contained set of innovations that were novel, ingenious, and brimming with utility—hallmarks of so many great inventions.

This book isn't only about Rob Turner, even though he is the founder, heart, soul, and driving force behind EMG and its success. It's about how, under his guidance and determination, EMG has gone from a garage operation to a large, highly respected, world-renowned company and how it has evolved, grown, and keeps working with artists to improve existing pickup/preamp systems. EMG also works ceaselessly to improve ease of installation, to broaden the range of instruments into which EMG pickups can be placed, and to keep advancing in a quest for better tone in a world of guitarists and bassists as eager to improve their sound as they are to keep their instrument visually and functionally close to its original design. And recently, after years of electric guitar and bass research and development, EMG has branched out into making pickups for banjo, violin, and experimental guitar/bass instruments, both hollow-body (acoustic) and solid-body, all the time working closely with world-class musicians, the people who forever pursue their best sound.

Whether in the studio or onstage, hundreds of thousands of instruments around the world currently boast EMG pickups. But as the philosopher Lao Tzu famously has said, "A journey of a thousand miles begins with a single step." This book covers that journey for Rob Turner, the inventor, and EMG's creation and growth. And like all journeys, there are unexpected notable milestones, incessant challenges, eureka moments, and hard-won victories. It also underscores Rob Turner's positive attitude and his willingness to listen to suggestions and to never let go of his deep desire to deliver the best products so that musicians can sound their best.

And about the book's author, Jim Reilly is not only a musician and educator but someone who knows musical invention and inventors, having written notable books covering two other important modern inventors in the musical field, Ned Steinberger and Emmett Chapman (*Steinberger: A Story of Creativity and Design* and *StickMan: The Story of Emmett Chapman and the Instrument He Created*, respectively). For this volume he spent over two years interviewing Rob Turner, his family and friends, and EMG employees and partners past and present, along with many prominent musicians and luthiers. He has done deep dives into EMG's files for details that were collected but were previously undocumented elsewhere. What you are about to read is truly a labor of love and appreciation. Prepare to be inspired.

Tom Mulhern
Former managing editor, *Guitar Player* magazine
January 2023

INTRODUCTION

A Brief Introduction from the Author and Alison Turner

This is a story about chasing tone, about finding one's sound and running with it. For the musician, it's obvious. There's a sound to seek, to discover, to uncover. That sound might be difficult or even impossible to describe in words, but when you find it, the heavens open, the magic flows. Guitar, bass, trumpet, piano, violin, or drums—the instrument is almost irrelevant. The instrument is the tool through which the player connects to that magic.

Stretching the idea of chasing tone a little further, it soon becomes clear that just about everyone has their own version of chasing tone. Once caught, one's tonal equivalent—the thing being chased—is undeniable. The sun shines brighter, the wine tastes a little sweeter. Art, athletics, business, religion, or relationships—I'd argue that there is a basic human need to connect with an individual and very personal interpretation of that magic where things resonate in harmony.

Rob Turner's story is about chasing the literal tone of some of the greatest music and most influential musicians of our time, music and the players who defined genres and generations. It's also about chasing tone figuratively and finding the right combination of elements to access one's personal magic while working with and for others to help them access theirs.

If you're not already aware, you're about to learn how the diminutive electric guitar pickup is arguably the most impactful link in the chain from a musician's imagination to an audience's ears. From the outset, it's important to know that this isn't a story about better or best. Although some will spend hours arguing for and against favorites, that misses the point. The point is not good or bad; it's about what sounds and feels right and finding what is right on a personal level. From a business point of view, if your "right" resonates with millions of others' "right," you're in pretty good shape. But often, the richer reward is found when one finds their perfect tone and nails that soulful blues lick to an audience of none. When both versions of what feels right, the broad and the narrow, coalesce into one and the same, we're back to that idea of magic once again.

This book isn't meant only for electric guitarists, or bass players, or even musicians in general. The story is universal. For the uninitiated, though, a basic understanding of the electric side of the guitar's workings is helpful. While many, many players have had long careers and made incredible music without any understanding of what's going on under the hood of their electric instruments, at this point, it would serve us well to turn to Alison Turner. She'll come back later in the story because she's playing a key role in guiding EMG into future, uncharted waters. (And, yes, she is Rob's daughter.) I asked Alison to give an overview of guitar pickups and to touch specifically on some of the terms that will come up throughout the book. If you're a pickup expert, feel free to jump ahead and dive right into the story, but even if you do know all there is to know, you might want to spend a few minutes and read on. I suspect it will be worthwhile.

Jim Reilly (JR): Okay, if I were to walk in off the street and say, "I want the Jim Reilly custom pickup," where would you go from there?

Alison Turner (AT): The first thing I would ask is, "What instrument do you play? Is it bass or guitar?" And then, "What are you looking for as far as the style of music that you're playing?" That's going to have a big impact. If you have a guy that's doing a lot of articulation in a soft-rock, fifties or sixties style, that's probably going to lead you into the single-coil territory. But then if someone comes in and they're a huge Iron Maiden or classic metal fan or something like that, you're immediately going to be like, "Okay, this person needs a humbucker."

It whittles down pretty quickly to the style of music you're playing, the tone that you're looking for, and the instrument you have. At that point, you're on to aesthetics. Like, do you want a metal cover cap or a white one? Do you want something that has exposed polepieces, or do you want something with a solid cover cap?

JR: *Tell me about the different pickup materials.*

AT: *Basically, you have alnico, ceramic, and steel. Alnico is a mix of aluminum, nickel, and cobalt [hence, Al Ni Co]. There are different versions of alnico, depending on how much aluminum, nickel, and cobalt are in the mix. Alnico 2 and 5 are the most common in pickups. The differences are subtle, but many insist on specific blends for specific purposes. Alnico 5 is the most commonly used probably because it's the most readily available, and it has a nice balance to it.*

We need to charge materials differently. We add a magnetic charge to alnico but not near as much as ceramics, which needs to be heavily magnetized. Ceramic needs the strongest charge but holds the most magnetism, so it has the highest output and it's really lightweight. Steel doesn't hold a charge. It just adds midrange tone to something that is already magnetized. So you never see anything with steel by itself, because it doesn't hold a magnetic charge. You're only going to see things that are alnico and steel or ceramic and steel.

With alnico, you get a lot of midrange and a lot of low end. With ceramic, you get a lot of high end, and you get a lot of brightness. On a spectrum, you would have alnico at the bottom with the most output and the most midrange and low end. Then you would have alnico and steel. Ceramic has a very clear tone. So, alnico and steel will have a lot more of the midrange. It's going to be your classic midrange tone. Next, you have ceramic and steel. With ceramic and steel, you get a nice balance between something that's not too bright but can still reach this kind of high-end tone if you need to. And then ceramic by itself will be at the top of the spectrum of high end and brightness. Those are the mixes that you're going to find the most: alnico, alnico and steel, ceramic and steel, and then ceramic by itself.

It's interesting, though. Steel can add a lot of noise. So you need to be careful. It can be very useful in taming an alnico-style magnet versus a ceramic. With the way Rob designs pickups, he can also tame those tonal responses with the preamp.

JR: This leads nicely to the heart of the story, the game changer and the legacy Rob's work will be remembered for: low-impedance, active pickups. Tell me about the difference between active and passive / low- and high-impedance pickups beyond the obvious that active pickups need a power supply.

AT: The thing with passive pickups and a high-impedance signal is that the sound is affected by so many things in the chain from the guitar string through the guitar's electronics, through the cable, and whatever effects are on the way to the amplifier. Any and all of these can alter the guitar's signal. One of the things that Rob always says—and I think a good way to look at it—is that the electrical path will always follow the path of least resistance. So the lower the value, the lower the impedance signal, the more direct and unaffected your sound will be when it arrives at its destination—it's not going to be impeded by anything else.

And with that path of least resistance clearly established, let's begin.

PROLOGUE
Friday Nights

I t's Friday night. In a little garage—actually, an old carriage house—beside a historic family home on a quiet neighborhood street in Petaluma, California, a group of guys edging toward the outer reaches of middle age plug in guitars, tune drums, and warm up piano keys.

Nick Sutton plays piano. His father, Ralph Sutton, was a famous stride piano player, one of his generation's best. Before joining the army and going overseas during World War II, Ralph played briefly with Jack Teagarden. His career took off after the war, and he became well-known for leading his own bands. However, he also played with Eddie Condon and George Wettling, among others.

Nick didn't see a lot of his dad while he was growing up, but there was enough influence that, of the three Sutton brothers (Greg, Peter, and Nick), Nick was the only one who ended up playing the piano. He never reached the same heights as his father, although that almost certainly doesn't bother him. Nick is a pretty happy-go-lucky guy. He's into yoga and pottery, and is, in the words of this Friday night's drummer, Rob Turner, "one of the sweetest guys in the world."

On guitar, financial-advisor-by-day Eric Abbott plays a 1962 Fender Stratocaster. Here's where it gets interesting. Years ago, Turner swapped out the original pickups for a set that he made. "We probably should never have touched it," says Rob. "We have the original pickups that can go back into the guitar, which is probably a good thing if he ever decides to get sell it." The guitar sounds great with Rob's pickups, though. More importantly, perhaps, the upgraded pickups personalized the instrument. The Strat now has "Eric's tone."

There's a bit of a rotating chair in the bass section. At the time of this writing, Adam Piacente fills the role with his Höfner Beatle Bass. The Höfner is safe from Turner's experiments. It's one of a handful of instruments with such a unique sound, look, and overall vibe that Turner thinks it's best left alone (more on this later). Sonically, it works well for the room. Even with its high ceiling, the garage tends to fill up with low end quickly if you're not careful. The Beatle Bass, especially with flatwound strings (Pyramid flatwounds, if you really want to sound like Paul McCartney, have a nice, woody, *thumpy* sound without much sustain that doesn't get lost in the space). Every once in a while, Bobby Vega sits in. Vega is a bass legend and lives nearby. He used to work for Rob (more about that later too).

This brings us to the band's drummer, Rob Turner. Rob is an unassuming father of two who has lived in the house beside this Friday-night jam-session space since the early eighties. He is a local business owner who has been tweaking with electronics since he was a kid in his dad's makeshift workspace. He's been into music for even longer.

In his late teens and early twenties, Rob tried his hand at playing professionally, but the concert stage never really called his name. That's not to say that he hasn't influenced countless concert stages all across the world. As he counts off his Friday night band to play their first notes, he hears the sound coming from Eric's guitar, and he can take pride in knowing that he is directly responsible for that sound. At the same moment, in literally thousands of bars, clubs, stages, theaters, garages, and basements all over the world, a very similar moment plays itself out.

On a thousand other Friday nights all over the world, musicians of all styles are plugging in and firing up electric guitars, basses, banjos, acoustic and archtop guitars, bouzouki, and even bajos both quinto and sexto. Some are famous, most are not, but all share a connection to that Petaluma Friday night jam band's drummer, Rob Turner: The longing, searching tone of David Gilmour's Strat on "Shine On You Crazy Diamond," Leland Sklar's soulful while simultaneously warm and punchy bass sound on any one of a thousand tunes; the triple assault of Metallica's Kirk Hammett, James Hetfield, and Robert Trujillo; Toto; Vince Gill; Béla Fleck; Lindsey Bucking-ham; Peter Frampton; and Prince—the list is nearly endless. Each of those players—and countless others whose musical careers hover a little closer to earth—found *their* sound, just as Eric Abbott did, through Rob Turner's EMG pickups.

For the uninitiated, pickups are probably the least sexy parts of the instru-ment. They're small, unassuming, and often blend into the instrument's body. But the pickup is the heart of the beast, the engine of the car. Take it out, and you may have a nice-looking piece of woodwork, but you won't be filling a garage, never mind Shea Stadium, with rock and roll. The electric guitar pickup turned the guitar from a folk, parlor instrument into one of the most important culture-defining creations of the twentieth century. Brad Tolinski and Alan DiPerna wrote in their exploration of the importance and impact of the electric guitar, *Play It Loud: An Epic History of Style, Sound & Revolution of the Electric Guitar,* "The pickup can be regarded as the most important part of any electric guitar. It's what converts the guitar strings' vibrations into electrical signals that can be amplified. A pickup to an electric guitar is what wheels are to a car. Without that, you're going nowhere." The electric guitar gave—still gives—voice to generations, has sparked revolu-tions, and has both united and torn apart communities.

Since the heart of the electric stringed instrument is the pickup, the quickest way to make a bad-sounding guitar sound good is to change it. By the same token, put a crappy pickup into that 1962 Strat, and you've got problems. Change the pickup, and you change the voice. Change the voice, and the instrument can inspire in entirely new ways. Voice reflects choice, preference, and taste. Different music calls for different voices, and a dark, slow blues is very different from a soaring jazz fusion. Rob compares pick-ups to paintbrushes: Some are meant for broad smears of color; others, for pinpoint-fine detail. Each has its place, so it's not a matter of making things better or worse but finding *that sound.* The goal is to find *your* sound—the sound that inspires you to pick up your guitar and play, the sound that leads you to your next song, that opens up the sky and lets the music rain down.

On January 24, 2022, Jim Lill posted a video on YouTube that asks the question, "Where Does the Tone Come From in an Electric Guitar?" Over the course of the video's eleven minutes and fifty-three seconds, Lill shares his experiments, changing everything that you could change on an electric guitar. He starts by comparing a guitar he put together from a hundred-dollar kit to his much more expensive guitar from a boutique builder. Clearly, the boutique instrument knocks the kit guitar out of the park. He then digs deeper and swaps out anything that can be swapped out of the budget instrument. He sets up both guitars as closely to each other as possible and leaves everything else—strings, pick, cable, and amplifier—consistent. In the end, the way to get the kit guitar to sound surprisingly close to its high-end counterpart is to use the same pickup in both guitars. He even goes one step further by getting rid of the guitar altogether and simply stringing guitar strings between two solid workbenches. He matches the string lengths and tensions, mounting the pickup at the same place on the string length and height from the strings. What is the result? It is best if you search it up online for yourself. Suffice it to say, there's an awful lot of influence in that diminutive, unassuming pickup.

Rob has been helping musicians find their sound since 1972, when he first attempted to create an active guitar pickup on his brother's Gibson ES-335 (probably another guitar that he shouldn't have messed with). Four years later, he and his brother Bill officially started the company that would forever change the sound and the way we electrify guitars, basses, and almost any other stringed instrument.

1

JUST A KID FROM SUNNY SOCAL

Rob Turner: *So how does this all start?*

Jim Reilly: *Well, it must be good for all. The publisher is on board. For me, this is a story about a builder, an innovator doing something new and creative. What I like best about your story is how, at first glance, it's easy to overlook the importance of what you've added to the musical landscape. But as you look a little closer and dig a bit, your sonic fingerprints are everywhere. The EMG story and the electric guitar pickup itself share the same persona. The pickup is the link between the instrument and the sound. It's the key, the linchpin. But when you talk to average people about guitar pickups, there's no real understanding of the significance.*

RT: *You mean a guitar player is an average person? [Laughs.]*

JR: *Right, but you know what I mean.*

RT: *I do. Getting that point across can be pretty tricky.*

JR: *But that's why yours is a great story. It's a creative story. It's a story about creativity and how the creative impulse manifests itself.*

RT: *I'm game. I think it will be fun. I have some stuff that I've written that I can send to you. The thing is that all the stuff I've written is pretty succinct.*

JR: It's all good. Let's get started and see where this takes us. We have no parameters or restrictions to really worry about.

RT: Good. Well, it was 1975 when I figured out that I needed to do something to make a living.

JR: Hang on, what were you doing before 1975? Let's go for the whole story.

On October 5, 1953, in Long Beach, California, Robert Alan Turner entered the world eighteen months after his older brother, William (Bill) Thomas Turner. Older sisters Pam and Dede rounded out the Turner siblings. Dad, William (Bill) Thomas Turner Sr., worked for the Douglas Aircraft Company. Mom, Betty Louise Turner, was a stay-at-home mom and, keeping true to the day's stereotypical nuclear family, ran the house. They lived across the street from the grade school the kids attended. On the surface, it was the picture postcard of the 1950s Southern Californian American family.

In the fifties and through the sixties, Southern California was booming. Jobs were plentiful, the sun was shining, and prosperity was in the air. It was a time of change as the rural farms and orange groves gave way to tract homes, shopping centers, and tourist attractions. Author Charles Phoenix calls it a "space-age promised land and the society that jump-started a cultural explosion." Knott's Berry Farm, Marineland, and Disneyland were all new and paving the way for an evolving society.

You could go anywhere and do anything, according to Rob. Long Beach itself wasn't small, with a population of 334,168 in 1960, but there was a sense of safety and community. Even though nearly everybody in the Turners' neighborhood either worked directly at Douglas, drove a truck for Douglas, delivered stuff to Douglas, or provided resources for Douglas, according to Rob, there was the overwhelming feeling that anything was possible. That sense of community and optimism extended into a common work ethic.

Born in Omaha, Nebraska, William Turner Sr. was brought to Southern California after his father was tragically killed in a car accident when the boy was only twelve. His mother, Alma, remarried and moved the family to Long Beach, where she ended up working as a nurse at the Long Beach Naval Shipyard.

Betty Louise Deloy was born in Long Beach on Lime Avenue. Her father was a tugboat pilot and her mother ran the household. According to Turner family legend, the Deloys came to the US from Ireland through France; Minneapolis; and, finally, Cresbard, South Dakota. In Cresbard, Rob's great-grandfather was the local purveyor of vice: he ran the local pool hall and drinking establishment. He had three daughters, one of whom, Margie, ran off to Southern California with one of the pool-playing, whiskey-drinking customers. Shortly after, the other two sisters followed, and all settled down on the West Coast.

Betty and Bill met in Long Beach at a USO (United Service Organizations) dance near the end of WWII. Bill didn't serve in the forces, however. He had applied for the Air Force but was turned away because he was colorblind. Being that it was a naval town, USO dances were common, and the young Bill Turner, looking very much like a young Frank Sinatra, swept Betty off her feet. By 1946 they were married, and children of their own quickly entered the scene.

As the young family grew, Bill Turner Sr. embodied Southern California's spirit, energy, and quest to achieve. Not only was he highly motivated, but he was also motivated to be his own boss. He worked at Douglas as a draftsman but was never satisfied being one in a room full of others surrounded by a dozen drafting tables. While he put on his shirt and tie every day and punched the clock, he was constantly on the lookout for a way out of the nine to five.

"My dad tried making a go of it with several sorts of products," says Rob.

> He tried to get into the oil-drilling bit business. I remember there were photographs of oil drill bits on the kitchen table. The oil-fishing business, where you go down to get a drill bit when it breaks or the line or the pipe breaks, was big. The oil business was huge around Long Beach and close to home.
>
> He also tried to start a company that sold electric lawn edgers. I remember seeing this orange thing with some blades on it. When you were in LA back then, everybody needed to have a nice lawn. There were actually home movies of my mom in a bikini pushing along the edger. But that was about the extent of it. It didn't go anywhere.

Eventually, Bill hit the motherlode by combining his love of planes, aviation, and electronics. In 1954 Texas Instruments, working in conjunction with Industrial Development Engineering Associates, released the Regency TR-1, the world's first commercially available transistor radio. In its first year, Texas Instruments sold over one hundred thousand Regency TR-1s. And although the sound quality wasn't exceptional, it changed the way that people could tune into the world. No longer did one have to huddle up to a huge console, filled with glowing vacuum tubes, in the living room. Sound was now portable and battery powered.

The transistor radio's design evolved quickly as demand in the marketplace took off. Very early on, the Japanese got involved. Masaru Ibuka, the founder of the Tokyo Telecommunications Engineering Company, was so impressed and excited by this American invention that, after seeing the growth and success in the American marketplace, he began developing and refining the radio's design. The Tokyo Telecommunications Engineering Company, rebranded as Sony, released its first design, the TR-55, in August 1955. In December 1957, Sony released the TR-63. With a nine-volt battery as its power supply, this radio quickly became the industry standard, selling more than seven million units by the mid-1960s.

Rob shares the following:

One of the great things about my dad, as he was growing up in Omaha, he was a model airplane builder. When he was ten or eleven years old, he won state championships. He was like the wunderkind of model airplane building. When he came to Southern California, he brought that with him. In fact, my dad built model airplanes until the day he died.

He was very creative. He understood plans and all kinds of things that went along with them. He actually built a plane in our garage. He bought an ERCO Ercoupe (a low-wing, one-seater designed to be put together from a kit). It came apart in pieces. You could take the wings off, throw it on a trailer, and tow it wherever you wanted to go.

I have no idea if or how he ever got a pilot's license—it was never a part of the conversation—but we were small enough to sit next to him, and he'd take us kids flying. I remember sitting next to him, and we'd do touch-and-gos at the Long Beach Airport. He skinned, painted, and finished this whole plane, then towed it over to the Long Beach Airport. There was this old German guy there named Schneider—Schneider's Air Service. It was the place where you kept your plane. He'd monitor you, make sure that your plane was in shape, and help with any repairs, that sort of thing. That was my introduction to airplanes and that side of my dad's life. I was pretty young, maybe six or seven. I vividly remember that the plane had this red plexiglass window at the top. It was really odd. We'd fly this thing around in the clouds.

Perhaps to support his love for those flights in his Ercoupe, perhaps just because of his passion for all things airplane, Bill decided to modify one of those readily available nine-volt transistor radios to pick up transmissions from Long Beach Airport's control tower. He had no real electronics background but did have an engineering mind and a fearlessness to get his hands dirty and create.

Modifying a transistor radio to pick up an airport tower is a relatively simple task. You need to adjust a couple of intermediate-frequency chokes (inductors used to block specific frequencies) to extend the radio's range. It doesn't hurt to change some capacitors and a resistor or two to pull in a new frequency. But at the time when Bill was experimenting, it wasn't common practice. It took a while and much trial and error, but eventually, he figured it out.

"I remember, as a kid," Rob continues, "our house always had two workbenches in it: one for my mom and one for my dad."

They'd make them out of plywood. The surface was a hollow core door. There was a shelf on top. As an aside, when we started EMG and we needed benches, we went out and bought hollow core doors, got some plywood, and made a bench—just like the benches that my mom and dad used to use. They were cheap, they were quick, and they were easy to build.

As he was working on modifying that radio, I remember going through my dad's boxes of resistors, capacitors, and all kinds of things, and thinking, "Wow, what is all this *stuff?*" He would work at his bench until late at night. He'd work at Douglas during the day, come home, eat dinner, and then he'd go into the den and work at this bench. There must have been an ah-ha moment when he finally heard somebody talking from the airport tower. He must have just gone, "Wow! This is it, amazing." There weren't scanners or anything like that at the time, and I don't actually remember the moment when he got it to work, but I imagine that it blew him away.

Almost immediately, Bill sensed he was onto something big, something that he could dive into that others would be excited about too. He headed out to the local electronics supply store (they were plentiful at the time) and bought a half-dozen radios and various parts and supplies. He bought a little twelve-by-twelve-inch hand-winding coil winder with a little counter on it and put Rob to work.

"I got paid twenty-five cents apiece to take the ferrite rod out of the back of the radio and cut the wires off the antenna and rewind it," says Rob. "For a kid in the early sixties, it was a ton of money. I was floating in dough."

The modified radio that could pull in air traffic control chatter took off. After three or four failed attempts, Bill had found a product that had some entrepreneurial potential. For a while, he continued to don the shirt and tie and head to the day job. Then on the morning after he received his pin from Douglas commemorating fifteen years of service and after an evening of celebrating with his colleagues, a bleary-eyed, hungover Bill Turner Sr. walked into the kitchen, dropped his pin on the table, and announced that he had quit Douglas and he was going into the radio business full-time.

Of those two workbenches cobbled together from hollow core doors in the Turner house, Mom's was every bit as busy as Dad's. Betty Turner's sewing machine was in constant motion, stitching McCall and Butterick patterns for the kids, her sorority sisters, and others in the neighborhood. "I went to the yardage store so many times with my mom," says Rob. "To this day, I can still hear the *fwap, fwap, fwap* of the skeins of material as the clerk in the yardage store unrolled and measured them for my mom."

"My mom had no fear," he continues.

One time, she took an upholstery class at Long Beach City College with her friend Sylvia Rogers. She was looking for somebody to go to this upholstery class with, and she talked Sylvia into going with her. So they went over to Long Beach City College, and I think they took night classes. She studied for three or four months, then pulled a chair out into the garage, ripped it to shreds, and started upholstering it. She got into upholstery because she wasn't going to throw out the chair that was probably destroyed by the kids and the dog; she was going to buy some new fabric and fix it. It wasn't just upholstery either. She could knit, she could crochet, she made stained glass, she painted, she played piano, she gardened, she did everything—it was amazing. She was absolutely incredible.

Betty shared Bill's work ethic: when something needed to be done, you figured out how to do it, and you did it. They passed this on to the kids. They were supportive of their kids, but their message to them was very much "You're on your own. Figure it out. We did, and you can do it, too." That adage hit home with Rob. Mom was also very supportive of Dad. When Bill quit Douglas, she was a little freaked out, but they both saw that the radio business held the potential to make more money than he could at Douglas, so she was all in.

As the business grew, Bill's radios evolved. Rob was right there beside his father and often accompanied him in the search for new parts and supplies. As the design evolved, in addition to changing the antenna and three or four components on the circuit board itself, he changed the dial to read the expanded frequency range. For this, Bill had to have a custom decal printed.

Rob says the following:

We used to go to this place that was on Magnolia Street, right down the street from my grandma's house. It was called Calray Decal Company. There was a guy in there that wore this big, blue apron. It was a print house. They'd print decals, stickers, whatever you needed. This guy looked like the guy in the *Mad Max* movie, who you'd give your guns to before you went into the Thunderdome, the guy with that big, round face with a monocle—that was this dude. I'll never forget him. He was scary, but he was truly the nicest guy. You would go in there, and he'd have decals like "Ed 'Big Daddy' Roth's Rat Fink," surfing decals, that kind of stuff.

I got introduced to the idea that when I needed something I couldn't make myself, I could always find someone to help me out. If we needed a decal, we'd go to the decal guy, or when we needed to advertise, we'd go to our point-of-sale guy. I say "ours" because I went with my dad to all these places. It was absolutely incredible—the people we'd meet—and at the time, I had no idea that they were affecting me.

It was an amazing time for me. People would come to the shop and say, "How do you know how to do this?" or "How do you know how to do that?" It's not like I knew how to do it, but I knew that this was what you had to do in order to learn how to do it.

Bill's radio business took off. His scanners became common stock in all of the little airports' flight supply shops around Southern California. Soon it got to the point where Bill needed a lot more radios. The Turner house was about twenty minutes away from Disneyland in Anaheim, California. Across from the theme park, there used to be strawberry fields owned by Hiroshi Fujishige. According to Bill, Fujishige was connected to Kazuo Hashimoto and Phonetel, the first importer of commercially available telephone answering machines into the United States. Bill connected with those importers. At first, the plan was to see about ordering radios in bulk. However, the discussion quickly turned to the possibility of building the radios specifically for Turner in Japan and importing them rather than bringing in the stock nine-volt transistor radio and doing the modifications in Long Beach.

"So, my dad flew to Japan," Rob continues, "and met the guys at the Tokai Radio company. They ended up making the radios for him in Japan, and he imported them. He changed a couple of things. The dial arrangement went from a linear to circular. He got a patent on the dial arrangement that he drew up and a couple of other innovations. He ended up traveling back and forth to Japan quite a bit, and my mom would meet him in Hawaii for a little vacation. You always had to stop in Hawaii in those days."

Radios weren't the only things making noise in the Turner house. The same spirit of freedom and innovation that defined the Southern California business world was even more alive in the arts, music, and the exploding world of teenage culture. The California Sound, with the Beach Boys and Jan and Dean at the fore, filled kids' heads all over the world with dreams of "California Girls" and trips to "Surf City." Long Beach fit the bill for both surfing and California girls.

Bill and Betty filled the Turner house with music long before their kids filled the house with "Good Vibrations." Not only were there two workbenches in the den but there was also a big stereo system. Frank Sinatra, Vic Damone, and *The Music Man* were in heavy rotation. On the weekends, Betty and Bill would go out to the clubs and dance.

The whole family used the stereo in the den. "We bought albums," says Rob. "We bought mono because they were $2.99 instead of $3.99 for stereo. My sisters were into music too. We had Frankie Lymon's 'Why Do Fools Fall in Love,' the Beach Boys's '409,' 'Surfin' Safari,' all that stuff. I was into dancing too. I loved to dance. I loved to listen to music. I became fast friends with a girl down the street, Jill Hutchinson. Her mom knew my mom.

It was all very clean-cut. We just danced and danced and danced, played 45s like Bobby Rydell and Wilson Picket's 'Land of 1,000 Dances.'"

The love of music went beyond merely listening and dancing. On Christmas Day 1963, Rob's parents bought him a guitar. He tried it for a while but didn't connect with it, so he gave it to his brother, Bill Jr. Almost immediately, young Bill was making music.

"He just took to it," says Rob.

It was amazing. Now, this was 1963. You can imagine what was going on, the Beatles were exploding. I didn't want to play guitar; I wanted to play the drums. When I was in fifth grade, there was this sixth-grade guy named Chris Meyers, who had it all. He was a good-looking kid, and he played the drums—you could tell he was a natural talent. I thought that if Chris Meyers could do it, then I could do it too. My mom and dad were supportive and insisted that I'd have to take lessons. I said, "Okay, fine, that's good."

We went downtown to Whittaker Music and bought a snare drum. The first day I went to try out for the school band, the band teacher, Mr. Zimmerman, said, "You want to play the drums, huh?" I said, "Yeah." He gave me two pencils, and he said, "Here, can you do this?" And he tapped out a rhythm. I tapped the same rhythm, and he said, "Okay, you're in." I'd passed the audition.

Rob played drums in the school bands throughout his middle and high school years. Often, he played second chair to classmate Mark Thomas. Mark's dad was the drummer in the Long Beach Municipal Band and a local drumming legend, but that was never a deterrent to young Rob. His parents were supportive, but they never bought him a set of drums. He always thought that one Christmas day, he'd get up and there would be a set of drums under the tree, but it never happened. As far as that dream went, the Turner maxim "If you want something, you have to go out and get it; you have to earn what you have" held sway. Working for his dad's radio business gave Rob the opportunity to earn money, but they wouldn't just hand it to him.

He finally saved up enough to buy a little four-piece set. "It was a Pearl set and not high quality, but I played the hell out of it," he says. "I played that set of drums until I was in high school—probably in tenth grade—until I got a real quality set of drums. But in the meantime, all I needed was that little kit, and I was totally fine."

With Rob on drums and brother Bill on guitar, the two fed their growing love of playing music by buying stereo equipment, turning up the music loud, and playing along with the records. Rob became good. Bill became *really* good. They played in bands with other neighborhood kids and got the occasional local gig. They built their own speaker cabinets because they couldn't afford to buy them. By the time they were thirteen or fourteen years old, they had figured out all the electronics and created their own sound system.

As they got more and more into playing music, the brothers were swept up by the amazing music scene in and around Los Angles. In the late sixties and early seventies, there was no better music scene than Southern California's.

"The first live show that I ever saw was Peter, Paul, and Mary at the Long Beach Auditorium," says Rob.

> The auditorium doesn't exist anymore. It was torn down because it didn't meet the earthquake code requirements, but it was a beautiful place, and the show was absolutely amazing.
>
> We played music with kids down the street, the Beaver boys, Danny and Bobby Beaver. One played guitar, and the other played bass. They were members of the Jewish Community Center. The Jewish Community Center had a bus, and you could buy tickets and see the shows at the then newly opened Anaheim Convention Center. One of the first shows there was a "teenage show" with the Doors, a band called the Merry-Go-Round, and the Jefferson Airplane. I was blown away.

The convention center officially opened on July 12, 1967. The Doors's show was on July 15. They played all their early hits, "Alabama Song," "The Crystal Ship," "When the Music's Over," "Break on Through," "Light My Fire," and "The End." Jefferson Airplane played "White Rabbit" and "Somebody to Love." According to reviews in the *Los Angeles Times*, the 8,500-seat auditorium was completely sold out.

Rob had been to other shows before the Doors. He and his friend Bruce Paxton went with Bruce's older sister to "The Teenage Fair" at the Hollywood Palladium. That bill featured radio-friendly pop bands of the day, like Paul Revere & the Raiders and Lesley Gore. That was good but nowhere near the Doors and not even in the same dimension as the show Rob and brother Bill would see next.

Melodyland was a theater in the round with a rotating stage, located directly across Harbor Boulevard from Disneyland's entrance. At the time the Turner radio business was still running out of the family home, and a truck driver named Elias would often make deliveries. He became friends with the family. Through Elias's family connections, he had ties in the entertainment world and would often bring complimentary tickets to Melodyland for Betty and Bill Sr. They saw acts like Buddy Hackett and Tony Randall at this theater in the round, which was only a twenty-minute ride from their house and an easy night out.

Rob continues to share:

One day Elias brought tickets to the Grateful Dead and the Jefferson Airplane at the Melody. We asked our mom if we could go; she said, "Sure, I'll drive you out there. I know where it is." It was not well attended. The reviews weren't great, but when the Grateful Dead hit the stage, our lives basically changed. They played *Anthem of the Sun*, and the Airplane did *After Bathing at Baxter's. Baxter's* is still one of my favorite records. So is *Anthem of the Sun*, for that matter. That just blew the wheels right off the train. That instilled in us that sense that this was the direction that my brother and I could go in. It was only a matter of time before we found other like-minded players, playing in psychedelic bands and having a good time. For me, it was the moment of liftoff. It was 1968. I was fourteen, and my mom drove us to the show.

2

LESSONS AT
EVERY CURVE

To all whom it may concern: Be it known that I, George Breed, of the United States Navy, have invented a new and useful Improvement in the Method of and Apparatus for Producing Musical Sounds by Electricity, of which the following is a specification.

My invention relates to a novel method of producing sound by the vibrations of a stretched wire in a magnetic field, and to the application of such method to various purposes, such as telegraphic or signaling purposes and for musical instruments.

—G. Breed, patent no. 435,679. Applied for
January 20, 1890. Granted September 2, 1890.

George Breed's patent marks the birth of the electric guitar pickup. In his patent application, he describes how a guitar or piano string passes through a magnetic field created by wires stretched between two magnets. He discovered that the string essentially becomes magnetized, and by vibrating, it causes fluctuations in a magnetic field, which induces an electric current into a conductor (Faraday's law of induction). It was crude, but it worked, and more importantly, it started the ball rolling. The first serious attempts to electrify stringed instruments didn't come until the 1920s, however, when electric amplification came along. Around 1924, Gibson engineer Lloyd Loar created an electric pickup for the viola, but it had a very weak signal. The Stromberg Guitar company released the Stromberg-Voisinet Electro in 1928. This combined a magnetic pickup built into a guitar permanently coupled to an accompanying amplifier. It was expensive, and the amount of volume produced couldn't compete with a banjo's natural acoustic volume. The first commercially successful electric guitar came in 1932 with George Beauchamp's "Frying Pan"—a Hawaiian-style lap steel guitar. It was marketed by Rickenbacker as the model A-22 Electro Hawaiian guitar. Their pickup concept would soon be adapted to hollowbody arch-top jazz guitars and eventually led to solidbody electric guitars. In 1933 with the Vivi-Tone company, Lloyd Loar filed a patent for a solidbody electric guitar; it was granted two years later.

In 1936 Gibson saw potential in the electric guitar and released their ES-150 Electric Spanish guitar. Jazz guitarist Charlie Christian famously brought the electric guitar to the front of the bandstand with this instrument. Les Paul took things even further around 1940, when he attached electric pickups to a four-by-four-inch block of pine, attached two halves of an Epiphone hollowbody guitar, and created the Log. Others followed until, finally, the electric guitar had evolved to the point where it was ready to take on the masses when Leo Fender debuted the Fender Esquire in 1950. However, in 1969, Rob and his brother Bill Turner weren't all that interested in the electric guitar's history. They were too busy playing rock and roll.

On the day after his high school graduation in 1971, Rob, Bill, and a group of their friends headed north, drove seven and a half hours through the Sequoia, Sierra, Yosemite, and Stanislaus National Forests and Parks, and landed in Lake Tahoe, at the border of California and Nevada. They rented a house and filled it with music, parties, a little pot, and all the other hallmarks of the early seventies Californian youth culture. As carefree as it was intended to be, it became clear pretty early on that they'd need jobs to keep the party going.

Luckily, even in the summer, jobs in the resort town weren't too hard to find. Rob ended up playing drums with brothers Eric and Ken Futterer in a group called the Nick Danger Trio. He was only seventeen, and although he couldn't buy a beer, there was no issue with him playing in the clubs. The band played six nights a week in the steakhouse at the top of Heavenly Valley, a ski resort in south Lake Tahoe. Eric, the younger of the Futterers, played guitar and sang. Ken covered all kinds of wind instruments: saxophone, flute, trumpet, and whatever other wind instrument he wanted to play. They played anything from Dave Brubeck to Trini Lopez and did their best to satisfy any audience request. Often, they'd stretch out on extended jams.

They were fed each night, which helped cut down significantly on expenses and kept things pretty comfortable for Rob. He made $250 a week in cash, more money than anybody else in their rental house. At the end of the summer, when Eric and Ken both left Tahoe and headed back to college, Rob stayed behind and rented a room from their grandmother in Marla Bay, an affluent area in Lake Tahoe. The Futterers would come back during school breaks, and the band would reconvene. One winter was enough, though, and by spring 1972, Rob headed back to Long Beach, moved in with his friend Mark Evans, and started working again for his father's radio business.

Bill Sr.'s business was going strong. He had transitioned from the airport scanners to amateur (ham) radios. They would import the radios from Japan and modify them with different frequency setups based on customers' requests. Rob and a couple of other guys would drive down to the docks, pick up shipments of radios, bring them back to the shop, check them out, make sure they worked, perform modifications, and ship them out to customers.

"I was working for my dad," he says. "I lived in this house on Falcon Street with Mark Evans, just the two of us. And that's when I started to get into guitar pickups. My dad would always say, 'If you really want to enjoy life, you don't want to work for somebody else.' Truth be told, I was bored stiff working for my dad, and I realized that I needed a product of my own."

While still working for his dad, Rob began the search for the product he could sink his teeth into. He had played around with guitar pickups and had started doing some guitar repair work, but microphones became his first stab at a product he could call his own. The deeper he dug into the microphone business, however, the more expensive it became, and the barriers to entering that marketplace proved too much to overcome. However, the lessons he'd learned taking apart and constructing microphones served as a solid introduction to capturing sound.

Next, he connected with a group of guys building a sound truck for a local cable TV company. They needed someone to build them a mixing board. Rob jumped at the chance. "They'd bought a kit mixing board from Opamp Labs," he says. "The guy who owned it was named Bela Losmandy. I'll never forget him. He was a total trip. He actually had a big influence on me. He had this shop upstairs at their warehouse with all these books and this little lab that he worked in. It was really very cool. He was an older guy at the time. I was nineteen and I was just really impressed."

With Dad's business having moved out of the family home, the shop behind the garage was open territory. Rob set up the traditional Turner hollow-core-door workbench and set to work building the Opamp Labs's mixing board. He also bought several Heathkit project kits and built all kinds of radio receivers, stereo tuners, signal generators, curve tracers, and ohm meters. Access to his dad's professional shop meant almost limitless access to catalogs, transistors, integrated circuits, and all the electronics one could need.

The transition to guitar pickups was just a natural fit. Guitar repair, electronic kits, dad's resources, playing music with his brother and their friends—the pieces were all there. The first guitar to go under his soldering gun was his brother Bill's Gibson ES-335 TDN (thinline, double pickups, natural finish).

Gibson only produced the ES-335 TDN from 1958 through 1960. The model drew its name from its original manufacturer's suggested retail price (MSRP): $335. Originally, they shipped with two humbucking Gibson Patent Applied For (PAF) pickups. The PAF pickups were developed by Seth Lover in 1955. Their humbucking design was Gibson's way of eliminating the sixty-cycle hum inherent in single-coil pickups. The design worked great, and the PAF sound is still one of the most sought-after sounds in rock and roll. Eric Clapton, Larry Carlton, Rich Robinson, and Dave Grohl are just a few of the players who've made the ES-335 a classic. A vintage ES-335 in mint condition with all the original parts can fetch between $20,000 and $26,000 today. To the right buyer and in pristine condition, an ES-335 TDN could be priced much higher. Of course, after Rob got his hands on it, Bill's guitar fell far below that coveted mint-condition rating.

"My brother was totally willing," Rob says.

It was a beautiful guitar. If it were in one piece today, it would be worth a lot of money. It was a maple top with a book-matched maple back. It had the classic three-position selector switch, two volumes, two tones. We took the pickups out, rewound them, and put a lot fewer turns of copper wire than you'd normally put on, and built a preamp to go with it. The preamp was just a single-input / single-output follower preamp. I mounted a nine-volt battery inside the guitar to power the preamp. I knew already that a pickup should have low-impedance output. These were just facts that were not only espoused by Les Paul, but they were also basic, rudimentary science. The guitar pickup should have low-impedance output, just like a microphone does. It should have noise-reduction capabilities that other guitar pickups simply do not have.

While he may be best known among guitar players as the namesake behind the Gibson Les Paul guitar, Les Paul's influence and innovations reach nearly every corner of today's music world. According to Sue Baker, program director at the Les Paul Foundation, Paul created his first musical invention at age thirteen—a harmonica holder fashioned out of a clothes hanger that allowed him to play guitar and harmonica simultaneously. From that humble beginning, Paul went on to be credited with both influencing the development and outright creating of musical tools such as the solidbody electric guitar, multitrack recording, electronic echo, and overdubbing.

His understanding of both the electric guitar and the recording studio led him to the conviction that a low-impedance guitar was far superior to high-impedance instruments, especially when recording. Legend has it that Paul went to the folks at Gibson and pleaded his case that all Gibson guitars should be low-impedance. They weren't convinced and reportedly replied, "We won't make all our guitars low-impedance, but [we] will make yours."

Whether or not that urban legend is entirely true, between 1969 and 1979, Gibson did, under Les Paul's direction, offer a series of low-impedance guitars and a bass: the Gibson Les Paul Personal, Professional, Recording, Signature, and Les Paul Bass models. These instruments weren't active like those with Rob's pickups would be. They didn't require an external power supply. Looking at the schematics of the Les Paul Signature model reveals that the signal from a pair of single-coil pickups went directly to a selection switch, with the bridge pickup going to a phase switch first. Perhaps the most interesting features were the guitar's two output jacks. One directly from the pickup's selector switch sent a truly low-impedance signal that could be plugged directly into a mic or line input of a preamp and then to the mixing board. The other output came after a step-up transformer, which boosted the signal to a higher impedance and would be suitable to plug into any standard guitar amp.

Paul himself was quoted as saying, "For years I've worked to produce a multitude of distinctive guitar sounds. The hang-up was to obtain everything in one guitar. Now, I'm not talking about gimmickry. I'm talking about the real McCoy—authentic guitar sounds, the type of highs that can rip your ears off, the type of bass response that's clean and clear. Every note must be balanced and offer maximum sustain."

While the Gibson low-impedance line didn't find commercial success, Paul himself loved them. The Les Paul Recording model was one of his go-to guitars, especially later in his career. Paul passed away in 2009. In 2012, the Les Paul Foundation auctioned some of his equipment. Paul's Les Paul Recording no. 001 sold for $180,000.

For Rob, the idea to put a preamp into the guitar to boost the pickup's signal came from his earlier experiments with microphones. He also realized that fewer turns of the copper wire on the pickup's magnets resulted in a fuller sound but lower volume. The preamp became a way to increase the signal from the guitar's better-sounding magnetic pickup.

"Any decent microphone needs a step-up transformer," he continues.

Without one, it doesn't really do what it was supposed to do. Without the transformer, it sounds good, but it doesn't have any gain.

At the time, I was fascinated by the *Audio Cyclopedia* by Howard M. Tremaine. It's a book that's about two inches thick (1,762 pages). It's one of those books that's organized by question, and each question is answered in sequence. All the questions are numbered, and the index is amazing. You could look up whatever issue you were having, and there was the solution. I read that book cover to cover, and I came away thinking, "Okay, this is the way this needs to be done." This pickup needs a preamp because I don't want to put as many turns on it so that I can get a better sound. I started reading about resonance and filters, all this different stuff. I was just totally inspired.

Other people would look at it and think, "This is just grueling." I looked at it, and I loved it.

As this was going on, the basis of the Lake Tahoe band re-formed in Long Beach. The warehouse at the Turner Radio Company became the jam space and the de facto laboratory for Rob and Bill's sonic explorations. People would hang out, listen to the music, party, and dance. Occasionally, the cops would stop by to respond to a noise complaint, but they didn't do too much and never shut them down. The players who would stop by—some, just for an open jam; others, more regularly—became the Turners' inspirations to experiment. A new guitar, a new sound changed everything and fueled the creativity. Bill's modified 335 had an amazing, clean sound and was a hit with the other players.

The band's bass player, Joe Martorana, offered up his instrument next. He, too, had what today would be considered a highly sought-after instrument: a Guild Starfire bass. The Starfire was the bass of choice for, among others, two of Rob's favorite bassists at the time: the Grateful Dead's Phil Lesh and Jack Casady from Jefferson Airplane. Those two players epitomized the psychedelic rock scene both sonically and culturally. The Starfire's stock pickup, the Hagstrom Bi-sonic, had a unique voice and, on its own, is sought after by collectors. The 1966 Hagstrom catalog states, "With the incomparable Bi-sonic pickups, bass and treble frequencies are separated, so that simultaneous bass and treble creates a new dimension in sound." The Bi-sonic was a single-coil pickup and one of the inspirations for the custom electronics that the recently formed Alembic company retrofitted into Jack Casady's and Phil Lesh's Starfires.

Formed in 1969 by Ron and Susan Wickersham, the Alembic company had started life as Owsley Stanley's workshop in the Grateful Dead's rehearsal studio. By 1970 Wickersham, along with luthier Rick Turner (no relation to Rob or Bill Turner) and sound engineer Bob Matthews, was pushing the boundaries of sound reinforcement and musical instrument electronics, most notably for the Dead and the Airplane, as well as the stable of psychedelic jam bands that the Turner brothers loved. Alembic saw the need for the increased sonic range of low-impedance pickups, too, and is credited as being among the first to successfully design an active onboard preamp directly installed into guitars and basses.

The Alembic pickups themselves were passive: they took the output from the pickups and added another coil in the middle of the body that acted as a nulling coil, which functioned the same as a humbucking pickup to cancel hum. The most significant difference between the Alembic active electronics and the active pickup that Rob would later create was that Alembic installed their preamp outside of the pickup housing. Rob worked his preamp into the housing, which made for a much cleaner, quieter sound and simpler electronic construction.

After Rob rewired Joe's pickup, lowered the impedance, and added his battery-powered preamp to the much-revered Starfire bass, next up for his modifications was one of the band's guitar players, Joe Hammons. Joe became a pickup aficionado and a stellar player who encouraged Rob to refine and develop his designs. However, even though changing pickups and modifying his friends' guitars was fun, there were still many miles to go before even the inkling that this could be the product Rob was looking for began to surface. He was barely twenty years old and nowhere near ready to settle down on one idea.

Not surprisingly, it didn't take long for things to start to fall apart with the young musicians' community that had organically formed around Rob's and Mark's Falcon Street home and the Turners' warehouse jam space. Joe Hammons had some friends in nearby San Pedro. Those friends were moving north, just past San Francisco to Sonoma, California. Rob and Joe and the rest of the ragtag musical crew were invited along.

They rented a big house on Broadway Street, right in downtown Sonoma. "It had a bunch of bedrooms," says Rob.

The place was huge. It had an attic that was big enough for us to rehearse in. We packed up everybody and all our stuff. I drove into Sonoma with Joe Martorana, just him and me. He had this old beater of a car. We must have been a target for the cops. We got stopped as we were arriving in Sonoma on the very first day, after driving for almost twelve hours. It was our indoctrination into Sonoma, and it was like, "Kids, you don't belong here." But there we were, living in downtown Sonoma, a couple of blocks away from the post office.

Regardless, it was great. At the time, in the early seventies, there were a lot of seekers, people from conventional companies, guys from AT&T, that kind of thing, who wanted to get off the grid and live off the land. They took a hit of acid, and they became different people. One guy had a newsletter with directions on how to drop out. He lived downstairs in the house we rented. We lived upstairs in the attic.

Shortly after landing in Sonoma, the gang started scattering. Brother Bill met a girl, Patty Burnett, and moved in with her. Everyone ended up needing day jobs because music gigs were few and far between. Joe and Rob ended up getting a job driving around all day delivering the *Sonoma County Gazette* newspaper.

"We drove all over Sonoma County," he says.

I learned Sonoma County like the back of my hand. We weren't making much money, though. We ended up leaving the house on Broadway and were staying at some friends' place. We were just about at the end of our rope as far as money and everything else goes.

We were out one night. We didn't have anything to eat, and so we went to the local Safeway in Guerneville. Somebody bought tomatoes and a head of lettuce. I put a pound of bacon down my pants and got busted. I got busted for shoplifting at the Guerneville Safeway! If I would have known that the Guerneville Safeway had more security cameras than God, I'm sure I wouldn't have done it. What was really sad was that one of the ladies that worked at Safeway was Joe's friend.

Anyway, I got busted and spent a couple of nights in jail. We sold an amplifier that we had so that I could make bail. Through my public defender, Gene Tunney (who was the son of boxer Gene Tunney), I ended up getting a job at this halfway house, bar, restaurant, [and] inn called Juanita's. It was this big, old, three-story house with a wraparound porch in Boyes Hot Springs— actually, in Agua Caliente. Juanita [Musson] had all of these wayward children working for her. I moved into this little housing unit that she had. There were a bunch of us there who were working in the restaurant and living there. She charged room and board. Nobody went hungry. Everyone had a place to sleep. You could do your laundry. It was a dream, actually. Juanita was hard on us, but I had a lot of respect for her, and I made sure that she knew that. I made sure that she knew I was grateful for her helping me out. Juanita's was famous for its prime rib. People would come up from San Francisco and all over, hang out, and even spend the night in the inn just for her prime rib.

Along with being a restaurateur, Juanita Musson was a local icon whose larger-than-life persona is legendary and lives on to this day. An equally colorful obituary in the *Santa Rosa Press Democrat* on February 27, 2011, reads, "Late San Francisco Chronicle columnist Herb Caen discovered Juanita in Sausalito and wrote multiple times about her overflowing personality and the eggs, slabs of ham and butter-soaked muffins that burdened her plates. Comics and other entertainers—The Smothers Brothers, Jonathan Winters, Bill Cosby, Noel Coward—made their way across the Golden Gate Bridge following late-night performances in San Francisco." Comedian Tommy Smothers is quoted in the article, saying that he found her to be charming, fiery, and fearless, someone he equates with the likes of writer Alan Watts and feminist/sex worker's advocate Margot St. James, and he goes on to say that despite having "the most intimidating personality," she had a naturalness to her without pretense.

The *Press Democrat* obituary continues, "Her patrons encountered a large, loud, soft-hearted though occasionally terrifying proprietor who gave free range to orphaned deer, a white pig named Erica, the woolly monkey Beauregard, roosters, cats, dogs, goats. Juanita herself said more than once she was no angel, 'but I ain't never turned away an animal that didn't have a home, and I ain't never turned away a man who was hungry.'" Her no-nonsense, what-you-see-is-what-you-get attitude and work ethic rubbed off on Rob.

"I spent the summer there," he says.

And I reconnected with Joe Martorana. We ended up working with this singer/songwriter from Sonoma County named Keith Stewart. After getting back on my feet by working at Juanita's, I moved out of her place, and we found this house up in Glen Ellen, this little, out-of-the-way, absolutely beautiful country town.

We set out to get work as a band and ended up renting this four-bedroom place with a library. It was at the top of a big hill, on Trinity Road. It was perfect. We could make as much noise as we wanted to. We could play. All we needed were jobs.

Unfortunately, once again, music jobs were few and far between.

"Keith got us all jobs planting grapes at the writer Jack London's ranch. At the end of the season, we got to play the barn dance. We planted grapes all day long, I worked at Juanita's in the evenings. It was a great time."

After the grape-planting season was over, the band kept living in the Glen Ellen house, and Rob stayed on, working for the London family as a gardener/groundsman and doing other odd jobs. "And believe it or not," he continues, "at that house on Trinity Road, I had a Turner hollow-core-door workbench. I had all the equipment that I had on Falcon Street. I had a winder, and I was still goofing around with guitars, pickups, and all that stuff."

Two other things happened while he was living in Glen Ellen, which serendipitously aligned Rob's musical cosmos. First, he met a guitarist who played in a band from El Cerrito, California, called Acme Express, and they needed a drummer. He started gigging with Acme Express in the local bars and clubs. They ended up playing the Holiday Inn circuit: set up in one place for ten days, play all the hits of the day, and then move on to the next Holiday Inn. This meant a free room, a half-price discount on food (no deal on booze, unfortunately), but otherwise, it was a young musician's dream. Rob was bitten by the idea that he could make a go at it playing professionally.

The next game changer came about six months after starting the Acme Express gig. "I got a call from Keith Stewart and Joe Martorana to come back to Glen Ellen," he says. "They said that they needed a drummer to play a series of gigs they'd booked in and around Portland, Oregon, playing at all these different taverns."

He needed no convincing, jumped off the Acme Express, joined up with his old bandmates, and headed further north. In Portland, everything changed.

CHASING TONE—
THE ARTISTS' JOURNEY
PART 1

Vernon Reid, Jim Root & Nili Brosh

A t this point, let's step away from Rob's story and take a look at a few of the artists who have found their sound through EMG. These stories are just a few snapshots taken along the journey of those chasing tone in the real world. While these may be just a few stories, they echo the experiences of countless evolving musicians. With evolution being the key word, some common themes emerge. More often than not, the journey starts with the young player just happy to be playing. As they grow, they start to notice little differences between their sound and others'. For some, those differences are hardly a distraction. For others, they start to gnaw away at the psyche, slowly at first, until one has no choice but to begin a quest for that ever-elusive tone. Soon, like a burgeoning wine connoisseur whose understanding begins to expand past merely red or white, the player starts to notice differences between sounds and starts asking *why*. Eventually, just as the expert sommelier can examine a fine wine and tell you the grape, the year, and even the side of the mountain it was grown on, the practiced tone chaser can tell you the type of magnet, build year, and wiring schematics of the pickup and why they like what they like. Sometimes it was a friend or mentor who turned the young player on to the benefits of different pickups. Sometimes it was a guitar tech entrusted to looking after one's instrument. Sometimes it was simply growth and maturity.

If you want the pickup equivalent of a lesson in wine tasting or a crash whiskey 101 course, listen to Metallica's first two albums, and then listen to *Master of Puppets*. Pay attention to the guitar sound. Can you hear the difference in the sound of the guitars? Choose your own words to describe the difference—the growth from the young, lively sound to the expansive, expressive, finely textured tone palette of a growing confidence and maturity. Obviously, there's more than just pickups at play in an artist's evolution. But I suggest listening to any of the artists featured here—or any artist, for that matter—and listen not only for the music or songwriting craft but for how the sonic texture changes, grows, and evolves over a career.

Like the mantra Rob has always held true to, this isn't about better or best; this is about personal taste and connection. It's about each person finding their individual voice. Sometimes it's undefinable, sometimes words can describe it—in all cases, when it's right, it's obvious.

This first "Chasing Tone" section features three artists who started their tone-chasing journey early, guided by a mentor, a friend, and family, respectively. All of them also continue on their respective journeys, ever inspired by finding, refining, and expanding their sounds.

VERNON REID

If you only have once chance to impress upon someone the soul, force, and power of an EMG pickup, I'd strongly suggest dropping the needle—yes, drop the needle on vinyl (since EMG is on vinyl) on Living Colour's 1988 debut album, *Vivid*. The first notes of the first song, "Cult of Personality," played by the then twenty-six-year-old guitarist Vernon Reid on his custom ESP with an EMG SA (single coil pickup with an alnico magnet) in the neck and middle positions and an 81 humbucker in the bridge tear out of the grooves with such power, presence, and authority that they pretty much guaranteed that the New York–based quartet would not be ignored. In 2017 when ESP introduced its limited-edition Cult '86 guitar—a replica of Reid's original custom ESP, complete with a version of the now-iconic swirling green, blue, red, and white design; a Floyd Rose tremolo; and the same pickup configuration as the original—the company went as far as to cite Reid as one of their most significant and influential artists and a key reason for their early success.

Reid first picked up a guitar in 1977, at age 15. He developed quickly, and after only three years with the instrument, he joined avant-garde jazz drummer Ronald Shannon Jackson's band, the Decoding Society. He would go on to play on six of the band's albums.

Living Colour's genesis dates back to 1983, although it wasn't until 1986 when the group truly began to gel. Mick Jagger saw the band at legendary New York music mecca CBGB and was so impressed that he had members of the band play on his second solo album, *Primitive Cool*, produced two demo tunes for the group, and was instrumental in orchestrating a record deal for the band with Epic Records.

Their debut album, *Vivid*, peaked at number six on the *Billboard* top 200 charts and sold more than two million copies in the United States, earning a double-platinum certification. "Cult of Personality" made it to number thirteen on the top 100 charts and won the Grammy for Best Hard Rock Performance in 1990—not bad for their first shot out of the gate.

As Reid's career gained traction, first with the Decoding Society and then as Living Colour was taking shape, so too did his sonic searching. Living in New York in the early eighties placed him at an epicenter for new music, technology, and changes in instrument design. Creative young guitar builders were taking on the established Fenders and Gibsons. Tearing apart stock guitars and rebuilding them with personalization unique to the player or piecing together one's own "Frankenstrat" from parts was far from shocking. MTV had ushered in a new musical era where fashion and style were equally as important as the music (some would argue *more* important). EMG was firmly rooted in this world, with Steinberger guitars and basses leading the sonic and visual charge with EMGs as standard issue in all their instruments.

"I started being aware of EMGs around 1984," Reid says. "I remember that there was all this excitement around hot-rodding your guitar, and after-market pickups were exciting. My friend Ronny Drayton was one of the first people to really move into this direction."

Ronny Drayton (May 19, 1953–February 7, 2020) was a friend and musical mentor to many. Reid calls him a very dear friend, basically a big brother. Drayton was a mainstay session player and an influence on many in the rock and funk scene in New York and beyond. His discography is long and diverse, and he is noted for his contributions to the Chambers Brothers, Nona Hendryx, James Blood Ulmer, and Joseph Bowie's band Defunkt.

In 1986, on 19th Street in New York City, ESP Guitars had just opened their first US office. Reid was a regular in the music shops along New York's famous 48th Street Music Row. As word spread about the up-and-coming virtuoso, Reid met the head of ESP's US office, Steve Kaufman. The two hit it off. The young company needed some exciting, young guitarists to help establish themselves stateside. Reid needed a guitar that offered, in the words of the ESP promotion machine, "the performance level necessary for his intense leads and funky rhythms." It was a perfect rock and roll match. Reid shares the following:

> When my ESP custom was being built, Ronny and I talked about pickups, and he insisted that I check out these EMGs. I was used to putting different pickups in my guitars, and a particular pickup in a particular instrument has a particular vibe. The EMG was a different kind of sound. It really gave a certain extra amount of sustain that was very attractive.
>
> It became my signature sound. The EMG sound became one of the signature sounds of that era, not just in the bridge or the neck position for leads, but also what was happening with clean rhythm too. I would characterize it as a very even sound, a very even response across the range of the instrument.

As Reid's ESP replaced his Frankenstrat, both he and Living Colour took off and never looked back. While his relationship with EMG and his love of that signature sound continues through custom guitars from Hamer, Paul Reed Smith, Parker, and others, he's not one to turn his back on other pickups or guitars. Rather, the vibe that the music calls for is listened to and honored. The instrument's feel, sound, and vibe all form and inform the music, and Reid fully understands the pickups' importance. He offers the following by way of explanation:

> I have a really old [Gibson ES-] 345. It has legit Patent Applied For pickups. They're not super-high output, but everything I put on it sounds great, any effect, distortion, or fuzz. It really has a particular character, and you know, it's also been aged in, too, and it's one of my favorite instruments.
>
> But then I turn around and I'll pick up one of my Paul Reed Smiths that has a thick, EMG humbucker sound, and it is just so easy. They're very different sounds, which are both very satisfying. It's weird to compare because they're really very, very different. Even if you have a guitar that feels good but sounds cheesy, you can completely alter it by changing the pickup. You

have to have a guitar that's resonant, though. If you have a guitar that sounds good acoustically, then you have a lot to work with. If the guitar is not resonant, pickups and phase switching and splitting pots are not going to help. The acoustic sound of the instrument still has to work. You have to have a well-built, resonant instrument, and then it's a matter of taste. Once you have a guitar that sounds good, then the pickup can make up the difference. You can't take a bad guitar and make it great—that just doesn't happen. The best guitars will always sound the best. But a lot of budget guitars now sound really credible, and some of those guitars can be made into fantastic guitars with decent pickups.

JIM ROOT

"This might be a little long-winded," says Jim Root. "I'm going to go back to even before Slipknot." Since 1999 Jim Root (or no. 4, as he's known to the Slipknot faithful) has held down half of the dual-guitar assault that, along with their current lineup featuring a drummer, two percussionists, a turntablist, vocals, a sampler, and a bassist, makes up the sonic assault that is Slipknot.

In 1995 percussionist Shawn Crahan, drummer Joey Jordison, and bassist Paul Gray joined forces in Des Moines, Iowa. After many personnel changes, in 1999, Slipknot released their self-titled debut album to overwhelming critical and fan acclaim. The album peaked at fifty-one in the United States on the *Billboard* weekly charts and was certified double-platinum with more than two million copies sold.

Root replaced guitarist Josh Brainard after Brainard had already recorded most of that first album. Since then Jim has been one of the main songwriters and driving forces behind the band, which has only grown bigger and more intense with each album. *Slipknot's* follow-up, *Iowa*, made it to number three on *Billboard*. In 2004, *Vol. 3: (The Subliminal Verses)* hit number two. *All Hope Is Gone* (2008), *.5: The Gray Chapter* (2014), and *We Are Not Your Kind* (2020) all hit number 1. Most call the band nu metal, some call it death metal, but all agree that it's about as heavy as metal gets.

"Before Slipknot," Root continues, "I never used EMGs."

I couldn't afford guitars that had them, and I couldn't even afford to buy a set. When I joined Slipknot, I can't remember what guitar I was using at my first rehearsal, but it just had whatever stock pickups it came with. It just wasn't cutting it. Mick [Thomson, Root's guitar partner in the band] worked at a guitar shop, and he got me an 81/85 set. I was using those in the early days. I was ripping out whatever pickups were in my guitars and putting in these hand-me-down EMGs. We started touring and we started getting some push and some endorsements, and EMG was right on board with us from the get-go. It was awesome.

Root used the 81/85 combo during the early Slipknot years. It wasn't too long, though, until he noticed that a 60 in the neck position—and the versatility it provided—was the pickup of choice for many other heavy players.

"I thought I'd try one," he continues. "It just blew my mind how bubbly and jazzy and sparkly it was. It had all these different characteristics, especially for clean tones. It gave me this really round, almost kind of brownish sort of tone. I dug it."

Like Metallica's James Hetfield and countless others, the 81/60 combination became Root's pickup combination of choice for many years. He even had Hetfield's signature Het Sets put into his custom sandblasted Fender Jazzmasters, but he found those pickups' output too hot, too overdriven. Tommy Armstrong-Leavitt, EMG's head of artist relations, had ensured that the relationship between Root and EMG continued to be strong and, over conversations about tone and different pickup combinations, suggested that they create a pickup that checked all of Root's boxes and captured his sound. Root took the offer and ran with it. From the beginning, the approach was to create a unique, custom sound.

"It was important to me not to just slap my name on something that already existed," says Root. "To me, it was not very creative and not like you're giving somebody something of value." With that mindset firmly in place, Root and the EMG team set to work.

"So, they approached me about doing this pickup. On my amplifiers, I crank the preamp gain all the way to ten. I don't have to use an overdrive pedal or anything like that, and I grew up learning on passive pickups—essentially, whatever came in whatever guitar I had at the time. With Slipknot, like I said, the passives weren't coming through. When you've got a DJ, a sampler, and two auxiliary drummers, everybody is singing, and there are two guitar players and bass, there's a lot going on and you've got to have something that can cut through all that."

Given those parameters, Tommy pointed Root towards the EMG Retro Active set. The Retro Actives were inspired by the seventies rock tones and the look of the Gibson-style humbuckers. By taking traditional passive pickup components and adding a preamp into the pickup design, Rob ended up with a pickup that responded like a passive pickup but with the quality, clarity, and power of an active EMG. From there Jim started tweaking.

I was lucky because we were in the studio recording *We Are Not Your Kind,* and I was able to not just A/B the pickups between guitars but could compare them in the same guitar. Because they're basically plug-and-play now, I could just—literally, in like five minutes—loosen the strings, loosen the pickup rings, just slap in a new version, and compare. We could also record and look right at the .wav file. We really only did three prototypes.

The main thing I did was have Rob back the gain off of them a little bit more and a little bit more until we got to a point where it was right on the cusp of having such low output that it was hard for me to get pinch harmonics, but I wanted to work for it a little bit. They still have great output. When we'd A/B that actual .wav file against an 81, it was soaring and it was just as loud, but you could see the 81's .wav file was way thinner than the pickup we designed.

They dubbed this 81/60- and Retro Active-inspired set the JR Daemonum set. "It just sounded so much rounder and fuller," Root says. "It just seemed to fill up the track better. Tommy was there that day, and I looked at him and said, 'We don't need to experiment any farther. This is it.'"

The Daemonum sets have found a home in all of Root's guitars, including his number-one Telecaster that has been on every recording he's done since getting the guitar. Where others would think it sacrilege to mess with the classic Telecaster setup, Root sees it differently, and both his Fender signature Telecaster and Jazzmasters feature active EMG pickups.

"I think a lot of purists probably don't appreciate that," he says. "But, you know, it's no different from Kurt Cobain putting humbuckers in his Jazzmaster or a [Fender] Jaguar. I'm sure there's people before me that did it. To me, it just kind of seemed like a natural progression."

The Daemonum set is a reflection not only of Root's sonic evolution, it's also yet another replay of the Long Beach garage scene, where player and engineer are ripping pickups apart, seeing what makes them work, adjusting and fine-tuning, and coming up with that personally perfect sound. It takes trust and a shared passion, and it speaks to the relationship and connection between EMG and Root and the energy they share by searching and growing together.

Root says the following on it:

> Honestly, I know a lot of artists always say, "Oh, I'm with this company, and I couldn't imagine being with anybody else." But for me, it's really true because they're so down to earth and so cool. They are just really genuine. You can just tell. The bullshit meter never goes off when they're around.
>
> I've been approached by other companies, and every time, they're like, "Well, we can make exactly what you're using at EMG." Why would I want that? I already have a great relationship with the people that work there, and they're willing to go out of their way for me. If I have any kind of bizarre request, they'll try it. You can bounce ideas off them and they're receptive. It feels like—and once again, this may sound cliché—but it really feels like a family.

NILI BROSH

The journey to instrumental rock guitar mastery doesn't usually start in Rishon LeZion, Israel. It helps if, like Nili Brosh, you have a family that has traveled throughout the world and brought home a wealth of musical influences and tastes. It really helps if you have three older brothers who fill the house with classic rock and metal. One of those brothers, Ethan, took it even further. Not only did he pick up the guitar and play classic Iron Maiden riffs but he also modeled the required passion and obsession needed to become a virtuosic talent for his younger sister.

"I come from a family that liked a lot of different kinds of music," says Nili. "I'm the youngest of four. I had the influence of brothers who had grown up in the seventies and eighties. That made things look a little different from what others my age heard at home. Queen and Pink Floyd—that was the stuff that was always playing in my house."

With those musical seeds planted early and inspired by her brother Ethan to play guitar, Nili was enrolled by her parents in classical guitar lessons when she was seven. It wasn't long before those devoted hard rock brothers and Nuno Bettencourt's band, Extreme, tipped the scales. She put down the classical guitar, picked up an electric, and never looked back. Synchronously, at around this same time, her father's work led the family to relocate from Israel to Boston, Massachusetts. Ethan was already attending the Berklee College of Music there, and Nili found no shortage of both teachers and musical inspiration to fuel her rock and roll dreams.

Public recognition started with a YouTube video: "Guthrie Govan Solo Played by 18 Year Old Girl (Nili Brosh). March '07." The video went viral. Her own studies at Berklee followed, as have gigs with Danny Elfman, Cirque du Soleil, Dethklok, Tony MacAlpine, Paul Gilbert, Andy Timmons, Guthrie Govan / the Aristocrats, Stu Hamm, Jennifer Batten, Gretchen Menn, Alphonso Johnson, Jeff Loomis, and the Iron Maidens, along with three solo albums (at the time of writing): *Through the Looking Glass*, *A Matter of Perception*, and *Spectrum*.

"My first electric guitar was a Mexican [Fender] Strat," she says. "Not a Squier but an actual Strat. It was a pretty good guitar for a beginner. I played it for a few years before I moved on."

Nili reaped the rewards of being the youngest in a musical family and following in Ethan's footsteps. "I am very grateful to my family for having been supportive and also having fun," she continues. "By the time I came along, they had the background to know where to start. I always felt like I had a sibling watching over me who wasn't going to let me buy a crappy piece of gear that wasn't going to serve me. My brothers just weren't going to let that happen. They knew better."

Her music of choice led to a fairly natural progression from the relatively good—yet equally relatively generic—Stratocaster to guitars that better suited her shred and hair metal leanings. The next guitar was a Charvel Model 4, equipped with active pickups (the guitar in the Guthrie Govan YouTube video). She played that guitar for several years before working through several other instruments and finally landing on the seven-string Ibanez RG1527 and RG927.

As her playing gained attention and her relationship with Ibanez grew, EMG's artist relations manager at the time, Chrys Johnson, reached out.

I told him about my experiences with active pickups. I was using passive pickups at the time. He was really cool about just leaving the door open and getting me to try things. He was very aware of what a player used to playing passives needed to get sold on actives. He set me up with the 57/66 set in both those seven-strings. I was really surprised. I wasn't expecting them to feel as smooth as they do. And I didn't expect them to round out the tone as they do. I did the A/B thing, recording with the original pickups, then right away swapping in the EMGs. I wasn't expecting to hear much of a difference. But the differences that I did hear were not what I was expecting at all. I've ended up having a long relationship with those pickups.

Brosh describes her signature tone as "dynamic, both if you're riding on the volume knob but also just in sensitivity in general—transparent, kind of warm, and not too high-endy. I still want to hear the sound of the pick. I think customizing a pickup is not something that I feel necessarily needs to happen, because the EMGs already are there. They're transparent, and they show you what's going on."

While the seven-string guitars will always remain a key element in her arsenal, Nili leans equally toward six-strings. Returning to six strings also means a return to passive pickups. Her six-string Ibanez sports the EMG Marty Friedman passive humbucking signature set with a passive S1 in the middle position. While the pickups are standard EMG, at Tommy Armstrong's suggestion, Brosh's pickups were made in a neon yellow to match her neon yellow RG550.

"It's the actual pickup," she says. "It's not a cap. That's the misconception. It's real. I think that's even cooler because it's the pickup itself. I hadn't associated EMG with a company that makes bright-colored pickups, but Tommy said, 'Hey, we're testing this out, and I think it would be cool for your guitar.' I was a little worried that it would be a little too bumblebee-ish, but I feel like it works. I'm really happy with that."

In 2022 Brosh added an Ibanez custom shop guitar, her dream guitar, featuring a basswood body, maple neck, a passive EMG H1A in the bridge position and passive S1s in the middle and neck locations (the classic Super Strat setup) in her signature neon yellow, a coveted Ibanez wizard neck, and exclamation-point inlays.

"With the active seven-strings and the passive sixes, whereas before I didn't even see a need, I feel like now I have a whole gamut of stuff that I can make work for different things. As far as EMG goes, I've now had a long relationship with the company, and it's beyond the products. For me, the best part of this thing is just how much of a family it is. And I just love being a part of that family."

3

AM I LIVING THE DREAM?

John Carruthers: The closer to the source you can get, as far as canceling hum, the better it works. So when you build a preamp right inside the pickup, you're as close to the source as you can get. The pickup is picking up the string's vibration and turning it into a voltage that the amplifier can see, and there's no line loss in the signal sent to the amp. In other words, the same signal gets to the amp that came out of the guitar.

When you have high-impedance pickups, that isn't the case. The longer the cord gets, the less signal gets to the amp, so you're losing a lot of volume. You also lose tone because the capacitance in each foot of cord takes frequency response away. That was a significant improvement, too. You could turn the pots up and down, and you didn't get that weird thing where the whole tone of your pickup changed according to the loading of the pot. The pots were only 25k, so they didn't really load the pickup much.

The other really cool thing was that you didn't require string grounding. You wouldn't get an electrical shock if you touched somebody else's guitar or microphone that was plugged out of phase to you. By not having string grounds, it eliminated all that. When you took your hands off the strings, you didn't get any buzz or hum. On other pickups, when you take your hands off, it starts humming because your body is the capacity ground that connects you to earth. That's what bleeds off the charge. If you don't have a string ground on a regular guitar, you'll hum all the time, even when you're playing.

Rob, Joe, and Keith pulled out of Glen Ellen in late summer 1974. David Bowie's *Diamond Dogs* tour was just wrapping up its East Coast leg, and the singer was about to take up residence in LA. The Allman Brothers Band and Doobie Brothers headlined the first Knebworth Festival in England, the Ramones played their first gig at New York City's punk / new wave mecca, CBGB, and AC/DC was about to perform their first shows with their original singer, Bon Scott.

On the *Billboard* charts for the first week of September 1974, "(You're) Having My Baby" by Paul Anka held fast to the number one spot with Eric Clapton's "I Shot the Sheriff" steady as well at number two. Lynyrd Skynyrd's "Sweet Home Alabama" was moving up the charts, sitting at twenty-two, while Bachman-Turner Overdrive's "Takin' Care of Business" moved in the opposite direction, falling from thirty-three the previous week to forty-one.

The Grateful Dead were getting ready to record what they were billing as their farewell-to-touring, five-show event from October 16 to 20 at the Winterland Ballroom in San Francisco. On the second set of the final show, Mickey Hart rejoined the band as the second drummer. The shows would be released in 1977 as *The Grateful Dead Movie*. Earlier in the year, Jefferson Airplane had transitioned into Jefferson Starship, and on September 1, they released their first album, *Dragon Fly*, under that moniker. The album peaked at number eleven on the *Billboard* top 200 albums chart and was certified gold for selling over five hundred thousand copies.

Meanwhile, Rob and the trio from Glen Ellen made their way north. They packed all their worldly possessions, including Rob's dog, a Rhodesian Ridgeback mix named Bruiser (who he had rescued from a drunk one night at Juanita's), into Keith's pickup and Rob's beat-up old car. "I don't know whether we followed one another, but we got there at pretty much the same time," Rob continues.

> We were planning to be there for three months, so Keith had arranged to rent a house for us. We didn't know it when we rented it, but it was definitely on the wrong side of town. We rolled up around 4:00 or 5:00 in the afternoon and unloaded all the gear. We moved everything—drums, guitars, PA—into the house. Of course, we didn't have any pots or pans to cook with—or anything to cook, for that matter—so Keith suggested we go to this nearby barbeque place that he knew.
>
> We went out, ate, and when we came back, everything was gone. All the equipment, everything we had moved into the house just went right in the front door and right out the back. It was just devastating.

While the body may have been able, the spirit was definitely broken. For Rob, who had never been motivated to play music for fame and fortune, having all their gear stolen within moments of arriving in Portland took all the joy out of the pending gigs.

"We still had these gigs to play," he continues. "So we went to this local music store on Riverside Avenue. The store was in this old bank building that had been converted into shops. It was one of those old marble bank buildings with an oak railing on one side where the tellers used to be. I'm sure it's been many different businesses since, but back then, it was a music store called Captain Whizeagle's."

Musician and Portland punk/garage rock mainstay Fred Cole opened Captain Whizeagle's shortly before Rob and crew arrived in Portland. A few years earlier, Cole had left Los Angeles both fearing the draft and frustrated with the LA music scene. On one side of the old bank building was the music shop. On the other, his wife, Kathleen (a.k.a., Toody), made and sold baby clothes. The band rented some cheap gear from Cole.

"I played one gig, and that was it," says Rob. "I was done. I couldn't do it. I said to Joe and Keith, 'You don't need me. You can just do a coffeehouse-style gig with just bass and guitar. You don't need me.' I was out. But I still needed a job. I still needed some money."

After a couple of weeks with only the bleakest of prospects, Rob ended up in another Portland musical landmark: Denny's Music. Denny's (which later became Old Town Music) was owned by drummer Denny Handa, who would go on to become Fender's marketing director.

"I'm not sure how it worked out, but I ended up talking directly with Denny," says Rob.

He asked me what I could do. I said, "I can repair stuff, amplifiers and all of that sort of stuff." So he said, "Ok, let's go upstairs to the repair shop." I went upstairs, and there was this nerdy sort of fellow who was in charge of repairs. He asked me a few questions, showed me some schematics, and basically said, "Do you know what this is? Do you know what that is?" He threw me a few problems and asked what I'd do. I said, "Well, you know, first I'd check this, and then I'd check that." He hired me on the spot. So I started working at Denny's Music. There was a pile of equipment that needed to be repaired, and they needed nothing but help. And it was great—the shop charged twenty-five dollars an hour. The repair guys got half of that, which at the time, was a small fortune. I spent the rest of my time in Portland working at Denny's and trying to get some money together.

The whole Portland experience didn't last long. By Christmas, Rob packed up, put Bruiser in the car, headed back to Long Beach, moved back into his parents' house, and went back to work for his dad. Bill Sr.'s radio business had been bought out by the Japanese conglomerate Yaesu. He had started a small research and development company that made various different electric components. Rob's job was assembling digital readouts.

Rob also enrolled in Long Beach City College, where he studied theater arts, math, trigonometry, and calculus. One of the highlights was running the sound for a theater production. He had signed up to do lighting but was much more interested when the audio tasks fell to him. After a year at the college, he moved to Long Beach State University, where he studied acoustics and the fundamental properties of sound: vibrating string theory, harmonics, resonance, wavelengths, and the like. Those were busy times for Rob. School, work, and that emerging passion for making electric guitars sound better were all fighting for his attention. His studies at Long Beach State only lasted about six months, as his other pursuits quickly gained traction and swallowed up both time and energy.

When not working for his dad or working on his college courses, Rob had taken over a Turner hollow-core-door workbench in the shop at the back of the house and started making pickups in earnest and doing guitar repairs. By late 1975 it had turned into a business, albeit a fledgling one, and in 1976, Rob took out his first business license under the banner "Dirty Works," so named because he'd do all the dirty guitar repair work that nobody else wanted to do.

Take the disappointment in Portland, add the skills he picked up working in Denny's Music's repair shop, mix in more than a little of his dad's voice telling him that he needed a product of his own, and add a little time and a Turner hollow-core-door workbench, and the climate was perfect for Rob's vocation to come calling.

"My first customers were a bunch of local players and friends of mine," says Rob. "Bruce Baldwin, who is still a very good friend, was one of the first. The first Stratocaster I did was for a high school buddy of mine named Larry Tramer. Jazz guitarist Ron Escheté was one of my first customers. He was teaching at World of Strings in Long Beach. Joe Hammons, who I had played with earlier, had come back to Long Beach, and he was willing."

The pickups that he had made and modified years earlier for his brother Bill and Joe Martorana were moving things in the right direction, but there was still much that needed refining before they were truly a professional product. And while the Dirty Works pickups were closer, in Rob's own words, "They weren't that good. They were definitely not what we'd make now, by any means."

Regardless, the wheels were in motion. This twenty-two-year-old kid from Long Beach started to make some pretty darned good pickups, and people beyond his circle of friends began to notice. "I pretty much just decided that this was it and that I was going to go for it," he says.

I devoted myself to this more than I had to anything before. I learned a lot about what other people were doing and experimented to see if I could apply what I knew to what already existed. Right away, I got a different sound. Most of the guitars I was experimenting with at the time were Stratocasters with traditional single-coil pickups. I'd take out the alnico magnets and replace them with ceramic ones, which had a different high-end sound. I probably ruined a lot of very expensive guitars.

So I started building pickups in earnest, but I wasn't really happy with what I was getting. They hummed, they buzzed, they did the things that I didn't want them to do. I had a really hard time with the background noise and sixty-cycle hum. It's like if you're trying to hear the band and a bunch of people are talking around you; it gets pretty frustrating. The pickup noise was just too much, and I had to do something about it.

I had a few books that I looked at for inspiration and finally said, "Okay, well here, this is the way this is done, and this is the way that is done. Why don't I try this? Why don't I try a balanced design with two coils?" I pieced together a design with a ceramic magnet and two coils, I plugged it into an amp, and I didn't hear anything.

I just sat there, dejected. Then I bumped one of the magnets with a screwdriver. The thing went *kaboom*! It almost blew me out of the room. Best of all, there was no extraneous noise at all. It was just incredible. I had the amp cranked. I couldn't believe it. I'd hit the jackpot.

Rob had reasoned it out, experimented, and designed a great-sounding electric guitar pickup with no extraneous noise. The next step was to sit back and contemplate the future, which is precisely what he did—but just for the rest of the afternoon. The next day he went back out to the workbench and built some circuit boards to go along with a pickup based on his new design. A friend of his dad's, Irv Cox, was hired to build the circuit boards, and Rob started making replacement pickups first for Stratocasters. Soon he ventured into other designs that would fit into other Fender and Gibson guitars and basses. Brother Bill was still up in Santa Rosa, but he was on board. Rob would send Bill pickups, and he'd sell them to the local shops in and around Northern California and the San Francisco Bay area. Add in a $20,000 loan from dad, and a pickup company was officially born.

"It was great," Rob says.

I had the plywood shelves and the hollow-core-door bench. It was fantastic. Those were the best of times, really. People would stop by and hang out. I was still doing amp and guitar repairs, but that didn't last too long. Pretty soon it became a question of actually turning the pickups into a product. I molded some of the first ones myself. The preamp was built onto a circuit board and actually molded. We poured urethane into a silicone mold, had them engraved with "Dirty Works," then filled that with white paint and tried to make things look professional. I spent 1975 through 1976 in the back of the house, basically just woodshedding. That's when things began to take off. We'd have a few musicians come to the house and check things out—nobody famous yet, though. We just sort of struggled along. We actually did pretty well, as far as sales go. I don't remember exactly how much we sold. It wasn't a lot. But rent was cheap living at home, and we just plugged along.

Everything was sourced locally in Southern California. Working with his dad had taught him about packaging, promotion, and the technical side of running the business. It was challenging to get the molding right on his own, so Rob found a company, Brand Plastics (in nearby Covina), that could injection mold pickup covers. Rob drew up a Strat cap and a humbucker cap and had them made. They featured a raised "Dirty Works" in italics. While the company name remained Dirty Works, the name of the actual pickup models changed to EMG, short for Electro Magnetic Generator.

Stratocasters were the guitar of choice for Rob's first EMG pickups. They were—and still are—one of the most common guitar designs, and while the stock Strat pickups are iconic and sound great in their own right, the Strat is a prime design for modification and personalization.

Rob aimed to combine the tone color of the early Fender pickups with added midrange and a higher output. The result gave the harmonics more of a bell-like clarity and increased the sustain significantly. He used a single alnico bar magnet to deliver a classic overdrive with a smooth midrange distortion, which kept the typical high-end clarity of a single-coil pickup. Using a bar magnet rather than the traditional magnetic polepieces gave an even response across all strings. Further, since the magnet didn't need to be as powerful as a standard Strat pickup's, the magnetic drag on the strings was significantly reduced, which gave them increased sustain. The Strat's single-coil pickups are well known for their sixty-cycle hum. The EMG's internal preamp cleared up all of that for an authentically noiseless output. Using a preamp integrated right into the pickup housing allowed the magnet to be much weaker, which also naturally reduced the generated noise.

As the naming and branding evolved, this pickup would be dubbed the EMG SA (Stratocaster-Alnico) and would, after upgrades and evolution, find its way into Peter Frampton's, Steve Lukather's, Kirk Hammett's, and David Gilmour's guitars.

This was the product, the personal business, the ticket that his dad had long told him that he needed to be his own boss, the secret to a happy life. The task now was to turn this expanded hobby into a real business. As great as it was that his friends and bandmates supported the product, it was pretty clear to all involved, especially to Rob, that he'd have to shoot for a broader marketplace. He hit the music stores and repair shops. Word of mouth spread quickly. World of Strings, on Seventh Street in Long Beach, jumped on board right away and became an important initial dealer.

All of the earlier dealers and sales outlets were important, but John Carruthers, who headed the repair shop in West LA's Westwood Music, proved to be the link that connected the chain and turned Rob's backyard business into the real deal. In the late sixties, shortly after graduating from high school, Carruthers moved to Los Angeles from Edmonton, Alberta, Canada, to help his sister train for the Olympics. Already a skilled guitarist and aspiring luthier, he landed a job at Westwood Music. Westwood was the watering hole for the best local players and a must stop for those passing through town.

Carruthers quickly became the go-to guy if you needed anything from minor tweaks to a complete instrument overhaul. By the time Rob showed up at Westwood with his new pickups, Carruthers had already done work for the Rolling Stones, the Eagles, Fleetwood Mac, James Taylor, Linda Ronstadt, REO Speedwagon, Foreigner, the Doors, Frank Zappa . . . the list could go on for days. The first player's guitar he put EMG pickups into belonged to Fleetwood Mac's Lindsey Buckingham.

Buckingham and Stevie Nicks had joined Fleetwood Mac in 1975. The band was riding high on the success of their eponymously titled album (often referred to as *The White Album*) and in the midst of recording what is arguably their most important album, *Rumors*. "We converted one of his Les Pauls over to EMGs, and he liked it a lot," John says. "That started getting Rob and Bill some notoriety. They were just a fledgling company, still working out of their dad's garage in Long Beach, but people figured that if Lindsey Buckingham had them in his guitar, then they must be pretty good."

Rob describes that early relationship with Carruthers a little more straight-forwardly: "John changed our entire lives," he says. "We would not be where we are, I would not be where I am, and we would not have gone where we went without the input of John Carruthers. We had a decent number of customers, but John was the one who came back to us and said, 'These are great, but they could be way better.' We listened like he was preaching the gospel."

Carruthers made many suggestions. Rob would send him samples. John would return them with his critiques. Following John's advice, they started using bigger coils inside the pickups, reduced the gain in the preamp, modified the bobbins to increase hum cancellation, and made a host of other tweaks and adjustments. Carruthers also understood the importance of the physical look of the product. Under John's tutelage the pickups' look changed drastically too.

"Their packaging wasn't very good," says John. The molds Irv Cox had made with the raised "Dirty Works" and "EMG" weren't up to Carruthers's standards.

I picked up Rob, we went to his original mold makers, and actually took the molds away from him. I had a friend who was a mold maker down in Santa Monica. He had his own shop and was quite accomplished. That's when we came up with the new packaging design with a textured cover and a smooth, rectangular, bar-type look with the recessed places where the screws went in.

AM I LIVING THE DREAM?

I had this embossing machine that I bought for next to nothing from a guy who was using it to make wedding invitations. You'd put the invitation into the machine, type in what you wanted to be embossed onto it, it would heat up, you'd put in gold foil or whatever else you wanted to use, and pull the handle down. The machine would push the type into the gold foil and bond it onto the paper. I used it to personalize truss rod covers. After a while, that got to be more of a hassle than it was worth for me, so I sold it to Rob and told him that it would be perfect for his pickups. That's when they started putting the little metallic inlays on the corner, where it said "EMG." They figured out that you could identify the different pickup models if you used different colors of foil. That really cleaned everything up and made it really nice and professional looking.

John became one of their largest dealers. He goes on to say,

Some players would come and say that they had a particular problem. Or they might be looking for a certain kind of sound. It might be that noise was bothering them when they were playing. I would say, "Have you tried these? Why don't you give these a try? They could help you out. Here's what they do for you. They fit in the same space. If you don't like them, then you can always take them out and put the other ones back." Once they tried them, they almost always kept them. And then, often, they'd bring in other instruments and have EMGs installed.

They worked really well for rock players using effects. Passive pickups get muddy when you go through processing. When you have a rack and you have compressors and distortion and some kind of flanging or echo, everything you go through takes a high-impedance sound, and it just gets muddy. You lose all your definition. With EMGs, because you didn't have line loss and it was low-impedance already, it was a perfect match to those effects. You'd have a clean, clear sound, no matter how loud it was cranked up or how many effects you were going through. It came out nice. That was a big plus.

With their cleaner signal, wider frequency range, and clear attack, EMGs were a natural fit with bass players. Carruthers put those early EMGs into Michael Anthony's (Van Halen), Alphonso Johnson's, and, perhaps most notably, session legend Leland (Lee) Sklar's instruments.

Sklar's main instrument in the late sixties and into the early seventies was a 1962 Fender Jazz Bass. "It was a beautiful, original Candy Apple Red '62 Jazz Bass that I found for ninety dollars," says Sklar. "I was in college at the time, and one night, I was bored and I sanded the thing down, cut the top horn, and pointed the bottom horn to make it look more like a Les Paul. I carved the whole body up and managed to completely screw it up. I had to put a two-pound block of lead on the end of my strap to counterbalance the amount of weight that I took out of the body. But it still sounded great. It's the bass I played on the early James Taylor stuff and on Billy Cobham's *Spectrum*. It has a lineage that's quite profound."

Sklar knew Carruthers through Westwood Music. One day the two started talking about building Lee a new bass. "I found a 1962 Fender Precision neck," Sklar continues. "Just the neck. It was an excellent, solid neck. I went over to Charvel, which made replacement parts for instruments."

Charvel was founded in 1974 by former Fender employee Wayne Charvel. In addition to building his own and repairing others' guitars, Charvel became a popular source for replacement and modified parts.

"They had a huge stack of P [Fender Precision] Bass-style blank alder bodies," continues Sklar. I went through the whole stack. I hung each one from a piece of wire and hit them with my knuckles. One of them just resonated beautifully, so I bought it. I went to John, and we decided to build a bass.

I don't really like the shape of the Precision necks. I like the profile of a Jazz Bass. So I brought in my Jazz Bass, and we made a template of that. John pulled out the frets and reshaped that P Bass neck into a Jazz neck. I was wandering around the repair shop, and I saw spools of all these different kinds of fret wire hanging on the wall. I picked up one and said, "What's this?" He said that it was mandolin wire. I said, "Let's try that." He said that it wasn't for bass. I said that I'd really like to try it and see how it works. I was coming from upright bass, and I liked the idea of a fretless bass, and this seemed like it would get me into that ballpark. I said, "Look, if it doesn't work, I'll pay you for a refret, and we'll go back to whatever would have been the norm."

He reshaped the neck into a Jazz shape and then put the mandolin frets on it. Since the body was a Precision body, where the pickups were sitting, we decided to put two sets of Precision pickups on the bass where Jazz pickups would have gone. But we were talking, and I said, "It seems really weird to me that on the original P Basses that the half of the pickup that's under the G and the D string would be closer to the bridge rather than the neck. Just by the nature of their tone, you'd think that just flipping them the other way would make for a more even, clearer instrument. The G and the D are going to read better than the A and the E anyhow."

He agreed on that. So where the standard Jazz pickups would have gone, he routed out space for two sets of P Bass pickups but reversed the position of them. In the cavity where the P Bass pickup would have gone on the original bass, we used that as a battery compartment rather than cutting even more holes into the body.

I trusted John when it came to the pickup choice, and he put in those EMGs with the big "EMG" letters embossed on the cover. I still have those original pickups in the bass, and they still work fantastic. We finished it with a Badass II bridge and one of the first Hipshot D Tuner prototypes.

It was either going to be an outstanding bass, or it was going to be a piece of crap. The potential was there, but there was no way of knowing as we were putting it together. As soon as we plugged it in and I hit my first note, he and I looked at each other and knew that it was a winner. John built a really beautiful instrument. To this day, it's still my favorite bass. Those pickups, those first pickups, when I went from standard Fender Jazz Bass passive pickups to Rob's first-generation EMGs, were a total game changer. Every time I'd walk into a studio, the engineers would go, "What bass is *that?* What's going on?" When I was in a full-workload mode in the seventies, when I was really working a lot, which was *a lot*, I would go through two sets of batteries a week. I would carry a voltmeter with me, and when I'd put the batteries in, they'd usually be around 9.3 volts. By the end of the week, they'd be down around 8.6 or 8.7 volts, and I'd just swap them out at that point. When that bass is really running hot, it's unbeatable.

I look at this bass now. I've worn the cover on the neck pickup down completely. You can barely see the "EMG" on it. The edge of it is completely rounded down, and there's a big hole dug into the wood from where my thumb sits. It's definitely shown its age. We ended up calling this bass Frankenstein. It was just all these different body parts that got put together.

Sklar says that he's used that bass on over 85 percent of the music he's recorded. And he's had a total of approximately 2,400 albums throughout his career, a career that's defined pop music for over fifty years and seen him adding the unique sound of his Frankenstein bass to some of the biggest hits by James Taylor, Carole King, Jackson Browne, Jimmy Buffett, Ray Charles, Leonard Cohen, Phil Collins, Rita Coolidge, Crosby, Stills, Nash & Young, Neil Diamond, Vince Gill, Hall & Oates, Don Henley, Linda Ronstadt, Carly Simon, Rod Stewart, and Warren Zevon, to name only a few.

Apart from the instrument's value for its genre-defining sound, the Frankenstein bass has become a priceless record of Sklar's career, music, and pop culture. He's collected hundreds of signatures from the artists he's played with and celebrities he's met over the years.

At first it was just a blank alder body. Back in 1981 I did a record after the Dodgers won the World Series. They immediately went into the studio and wanted to cut Queen's "We Are the Champions" and "Big Blue Wrecking Crew." There were maybe six of the Dodgers, [drummer] Jeff Porcaro, me, and a bunch of other studio players in the room. At the end of the session, the Dodgers were signing some baseballs. I grabbed a couple of baseballs, but then I said, "Hey, why don't you sign my bass?" They said, "Really?" I said, "Yeah." So they autographed the body because the body had nothing on it.

Then after that, I was doing a gig with James Taylor in Pittsburgh. Rocky Bleier and Lynn Swann from the Pittsburg Steelers football team were at the gig. They were backstage. They saw the bass and said, "Baseball players are pussies. You need football players on there." So they signed it, and after that, it just took off. I've got everybody from Sting and Clapton to George Lucas and Peter Max, Andy Griffith. I've probably got at least four hundred signatures on that body. Beyond just the sound of it, it has this meaning for me that supersedes any other instrument I have, just because of the history that's on it.

The pieces were falling into place for EMG. Some of the most significant players in the music industry, particularly in Southern California, were using EMG products. The most trusted repair shops and custom builders were pushing EMG, and players were showing up on the biggest stages playing guitars and basses with that big EMG lettering molded into their pickup covers. Studio players loved the clean sound, and soon, producers and engineers asked for guitars and basses with EMG pickups by name. Rob and Bill were still a couple of kids, though, and had much to learn before they would cement their sound firmly into the musical lexicon.

4

FROM COAST TO COAST AND ACROSS THE SEAS

Hap Kuffner: *We didn't make an enemy in the pickup business. We had friendly competitors. EMG was different anyway. We were not going after the vintage guitar market; our market was a whole other group of artists. We'd say, "If you're going to go onstage playing in front of thirty thousand people, that's awesome. We've got you covered. Any length of cable—no problem. When you touch the microphone, you're not going to get a shock, you're not going to get hurt. Any length of cable, wireless, everything is gonna work. And you can get whatever sound you want. You can play clean, and you can get a vicious wall of Marshalls sound, heavily overdriven." It was the same thing on bass: "We can take care of you."*

The best part was that if you couldn't afford a $4,000 Steinberger instrument, you could get exactly the same pickup and have the same engine. It was like dropping a Corvette engine into an old Toyota. That thing's gonna take off, right? So if you had a P Bass, okay, put these in there. Here's the Jazz Bass set. A PJ set? No problem. Here's a Strat set. Here's your Tele set. The humbuckers were a little slower to take off than the other stuff at first, but that Tele stuff, Rob's Tele pickups, are still some of the best-sounding Tele pickups you can get.

As the seventies turned into the eighties, the core of the EMG lineup had taken shape. With John Carruthers's mentorship and the feedback from an ever-increasingly impressive group of artists who were making some of the most inspired and successful music of the day, the foundation for Rob's EMG product line had found solid ground.

According to Rob, 1979 was a total reboot. "We were ready to listen to what others had to say. The other thing we needed was to make the product less expensive to manufacture. That was a big part of the whole redesign. It was pretty much Bill and me sitting around, grabbing a couple of cups of coffee or a bottle of wine and saying, 'Let's figure out what direction we really want to go. Who do we listen to? How do we attack this thing? How do we get to the next level?'"

The EMG SA, which began life in 1974 as the first noiseless single-coil pickup, combined the early Stratocaster sound's attributes with added midrange response and a higher output. Clear, defined, ringing harmonics and overtones and much greater sustain than a passive single-coil gave the SA far more versatility than traditional single-coil pickups. A single alnico bar magnet delivered a classic-sounding overdrive with smooth midrange distortion while still managing to retain a single-coil pickup's familiar high-end response. The internal preamp eliminated the sixty-cycle hum of a passive single-coil. The EMG S'shared the same features as the SA, only it replaced the alnico magnet with a ceramic one, giving that version a brighter tone.

This lineup also featured the H model, which was EMG's original single-coil pickup design in a humbucker housing. The EMG H featured a wider frequency response range than the pickups that had come before, resulting in a unique clarity and a richer blend of harmonics. The EMG HA came on board shortly thereafter. This was virtually the same design as the H but with an alnico magnet rather than ceramic, for added warmth. The H and HA models were built into humbucking housings for Ted Newman Jones, a guitar builder in Austin, Texas. Jones needed a pickup that didn't have polepieces for the Rolling Stones' Keith Richards, who wanted a single-coil sound in a humbucker housing for his modified five-string Telecaster-style guitars. For the rhythm guitarist looking for added definition for chording, either pickup worked well. For lead work, when the bright attack of a single-coil pickup was called for, the added bite of the H did the trick. The Newman guitars were outfitted with the H in the rhythm position and the HA in the bridge.

The EMG 58 was Rob's take on the classic Gibson P-90 pickup and that bright, transparent Gibson sound. It featured an alnico magnet with two steel bars. The original 58 design was noisier than Rob liked. It was replaced by the EMG 85, which has gone on to become one of the go-to EMGs in either the bridge or rhythm position.

Developed in 1979 but released in 1981, the EMG 81 was designed for the high-output lead guitarist. Rather than polepieces, the 81 had steel bars and a ceramic magnet. The sound could cut through a mix, be colored with distortion and effects without becoming muddy, and, perhaps best of all, was truly noiseless. Soon guitars with a 58/85 in the neck position (for rhythm) and an 81 in the bridge (for lead) became a signature rock combination.

On bass, the original pickups with the embossed EMG logo had already been heard on countless recordings by players like Leland Sklar, Alphonso Johnson, Van Halen's Michael Anthony, and Kiss's Gene Simmons. The clear, cutting bass sound with the extended frequency response provided a foundation that was hard to beat. The updated EMG P used short, squat coils with very little resistance, wired in parallel, resulting in about twice as much low end as earlier passive pickups. Ceramic magnets were the magnets of choice for their added clarity.

Over the years updated and modified versions of these pickups, along with entirely new designs, have joined the EMG roster. However, it's safe to say that EMG had found their footing and a solid base with the above lineup, and whether they knew it or not, they were about to jump from that rock-solid foundation and into the stratosphere.

Company name changes followed suit. The company had started life as Dirty Works Studio. In 1978 they became Overlend, to reflect their far-extended credit situation. The product had always been called EMG, though, and that's how they were known in the industry. In 1983 they simplified, acquiesced, and formally changed the business license to read "EMG."

The stars were aligning for EMG. The music scene was changing as the eighties were ushering in a new era of overdriven rock and virtuoso pop musicianship. Also, those behind the scenes in the guitar and bass business saw the commercial potential in Rob's designs and wanted to be a part of it. Add to that a growing DIY mentality that gave permission for players to modify, tweak, cut up, and personalize their instruments—the most famous and influential guitar player of the day, Eddie Van Halen, had cobbled together his most iconic instrument from parts—and you've got the perfect musical storm.

Hand in hand with advances in technology and the musical instrument-manufacturing industry's growth, the musical world itself was shrinking. Both players and instrument manufacturers from the United States, across Europe, and throughout Asia were reciprocally influencing each other, sometimes even blurring copyright lines.

During the seventies and into the eighties, the Japanese guitar-manufacturing industry thrived. However, it was a contentious time, as a significant number of Japanese companies made nearly identical copies of American Fenders and Gibsons. In 1978 Gibson sued the Japanese company Ibanez, claiming copyright infringement and coining the term *lawsuit guitars* to define those too-close copies. As a result, Ibanez and others changed their designs, and some evolved into significant music-industry players in their own right. Fernandes, Tokai, Greco, Yamaha, and Westminster were among those Japanese companies who either followed suit and modified their designs or faded away.

Ironically, many feel that the American instruments' quality had declined significantly in the seventies, and many of these Japanese guitars actually outperformed their US inspirations. Taking that one step further, some argue that pressure from that overseas competition led to a revitalization of the US instrument-making industry. Regardless, American musicians and music heavily influenced Japanese culture, especially among the youth, and those young musicians wanted both that American sound and look.

In 1978 Tatsuo Okada was studying anthropology at the University of California and playing guitar in a couple of San Francisco Bay Area bands. The bass player in one of his bands had started a musical instrument import-export business that shipped gear back and forth from the United States to Japan. Okada shares the following:

> At that time, the Japanese product was so strong both in terms of pricing and quality that Japanese instruments were really taking over the market. But I was seeing so many good US instruments at the time, as well, and I thought: "Why is everything coming from Japan? Why not sell it the other way?" Although it was expensive, based on exchange rates, I figured that since I played American guitars and liked them, there had to be people in Japan

who would like them too. I kind of went against the grain of the period. At that time, I was more into sending American instruments and related musical items to Japan rather than importing from there.

Based both on the mindset that there was a marketplace for American musical products and Tatsuo's growing reputation back in Japan, Mr. Hats Fujitani, the chief guitar engineer at the Fernandes Guitar company, reached out to Tatsuo and asked him to check out EMG pickups. That request started a relationship that's lasted over forty years.

"That's why I first connected with Rob," Tatsuo continues.

When I visited him for the first time, I still vividly remember it: he and Bill were working in a small garage. They were both winding coils themselves. I told them that Fernandes really loved EMG and wanted me to supply them. But at that time, EMG couldn't make as many pickups as Mr. Fujitani wanted. Rob basically said, "Here's what I can do for you. If that's okay with you, we can do business together." I called Mr. Fujitani, and he said, "That's okay. Whatever they can supply, we'll buy." That was how it all started, and it continued like that with Rob supplying as many pickups as he could for the first couple of years.

At the time, the Japanese economy was very strong. According to Okada, work was plentiful for studio musicians, and they didn't mind paying a premium for top-of-the-line gear. Those studio players were being heavily influenced by the American session players and the innovative, fresh crop of jazz-influenced rock bands who were starting to hit the charts. Lee Sklar's playing was no stranger to the Japanese, but even more influential on the guitar side was a young Californian guitarist named Steve Lukather. Lukather's band, Toto, had charted internationally with their first two albums, *Toto* (1978) and *Hydra* (1979). Songs like "Hold the Line," "I'll Supply the Love," and "99" became both AM and FM radio staples. On both of those albums, Lukather liberally employed one of his custom EMG-equipped Valley Arts guitars, made by luthier Mike McGuire.

"Japanese players really liked that sound," Tatsuo continues. "The quality of the product was excellent and consistent too. That good sound and good quality established the EMG name in Japan."

In 1982 Tatsuo founded Okada International and became the exclusive distributor of EMG pickups in Asia, a relationship that continues to this day.

Over all those years, Okada says that Rob's business style hasn't changed. In 1992 Okada established a US division of Fernandes Guitars. Fernandes US became known for custom-built instruments and the Sustainer pickup system, which created an infinitely sustaining guitar note. Although they'd use several different pickup brands, EMG was by far the most requested choice. Japanese bands Loudness, Buck-Tick, X Japan, and D'erlanger feature EMG-equipped guitars and basses. Players such as Metallica's Robert Trujillo and Kirk Hammett, Brad Gillis from Night Ranger and Ozzy Osbourne's band, Steve Hackett, Todd Rundgren, and Peter Frampton are a few Fernandes players more familiar to North American audiences.

"Before EMGs, there was no pickup that was so quiet yet, at the same time, had a tone that was so rich," Okada says. "That was the biggest impression on our market. You could get a distortion sound but with no noise. Before that, distortion sound with a passive pickup was always noisy. I believe, and I may be exaggerating, but I think that lots of people were inspired to play with a clean sound because of the EMG sound. They liked they could get both a rich, clean sound yet, at the same time, a really elegant fuzz tone from one pickup."

Back stateside, John Carruthers wasn't the only influential Southern Californian luthier singing the praises of EMG pickups. Mike McGuire grew up taking guitar lessons, along with his friend Al Carness, at Duke Miller's North Hollywood music store. The two were a fixture at Miller's. By fifteen, McGuire was teaching there himself. In late 1969, after a four-year stint in the US Navy, McGuire returned to Los Angeles, where he and Carness bought out Duke and took over the day-to-day store operations.

"We were both teaching and running this very small store," McGuire says.

We would sell one guitar and buy two. Then we'd sell two and buy four—you know, that kind of thing. We just built it up like that. I don't remember the exact date that we changed the name to Valley Arts, but we did. Around that same time, I started working and studying guitar repair with Jack Willock in Glendale, who was probably the number-one guitar repair guy in the country at the time. I'd sweep the floors a little bit in the morning, and then he'd show me something or other. I remember my first fret job. It was a bass neck, and I botched it horribly. I ran it over to Jack. Of course, he had a magic hammer that he put frets in with, and he bailed me out. His was a beautiful fret job. That's how I started my guitar repair career, and I just kept going.

The name change from Duke Miller's to Valley Arts wasn't the only change Mike and Al made. They relocated from Laurel Canyon to Ventura Boulevard in Studio City. The store was much bigger and in the heart of the Los Angeles music and entertainment industry. Al took the lead, managing the teaching staff and most of the business aspects. Mike handled sales and repairs. He had a little window in the repair shop that looked out into the store. If a customer came in while he was working on an instrument, he'd run out from behind his workbench and take care of them. As his guitar repair skills and reputation grew, more and more of the big-name studio players and heavyweight musicians called on his services. Larry Carlton was one of the first significant players to discover Valley Arts Guitar Shop. Soon Tommy Tedesco, Steve Lukather, Robben Ford, Mitch Holder, Mundell Lowe, Al Viola, Duane Eddy, Lee Ritenour, and many others became regulars.

Around 1977 McGuire started exploring building his own guitars. The first was basically a Stratocaster copy with a quilted maple body and an ebony fingerboard. Rumor has it that Larry Carlton ended up with the guitar. "I did it basically to see if I could, and it sold right away," he says. "I figured that wasn't such a bad deal." By 1979 he had become a serious luthier, and Valley Arts Guitars was born.

Steve Lukather turned Mike on to EMG pickups. Mike goes on to say,

He was just starting his recording career and was already a very good player. He wanted a good, strong, clean signal to hit his pedalboard. The EMG sound simply was superior. It had a very strong signal, virtually no noise, no static, no ground problems, none of that stuff, which is always a problem with single-coil pickups. Once people started using them and seeing more of them around, it just mushroomed from there, and they became the go-to pickup for Valley Arts. We still used other brands, but the EMG pickup became our most popular. Eventually, we did a Lukather signature model with two EMG SAs and an 85. EMGs really took off after that signature model. I remember the first time Larry Carlton played a guitar I built for him with EMG pickups. He loved it too.

Lukather's Valley Arts guitars became a fixture in concerts, on the groundbreaking Toto albums, and on countless recording sessions.

In the early nineties, Lee Sklar had McGuire replicate the bass John Carruthers had built for him back in the very early days of EMG. "He wanted the same exact sound," says McGuire, "or as close as he could get. I asked him about the preamp with the two nine-volt batteries. I said, 'What the heck is that for? You know, it's already a powerful signal.' He said, 'Well, it gives me more headroom,' or something like that. I called Rob. We talked about it, and he said that they didn't build them like that anymore. But he built one for me anyway, and it was fabulous. It sounded great. Lee was very happy."

In an open letter addressed to "All My Fellow Musicians," Sklar writes, "I have worked in LA for many years and have dealt with many music stores and repair shops. The relationship I have developed with Valley Arts is by far the most productive and enjoyable. From the first time I walked into the store, Al and Mike and all the staff have made me feel at home and that they genuinely care that my needs are covered. It is my first stop and first choice, and I highly recommend the same to all of you."

Steve Lukather's influence looms large with musicians throughout those critical early EMG days, as Bill and Rob were taking the company from a small, family-run business to an international powerhouse. However, while names like Lee Sklar, Larry Carlton, and Lukather were on the tip of guitar and bass players' tongues, they weren't the ones standing centerstage. Peter Frampton would take EMG from the sidelines into the spotlight, although not without some help from Lukather.

Jon (J. D.) Dworkow calls himself a "rock and roll janitor." A much less humble resume reads stage manager, crew chief, and backline technician for, among others, Prince, Billy Idol, Bon Jovi, and the Rolling Stones. For a brief time, he was the director of Artists Relations at Fender. He also worked on significant concert events, including Live Aid, Grammy telecasts, and Eric Clapton's Crossroads Guitar Festival.

In 1980 he went to work for Peter Frampton and was part of Frampton's infamous South American tour. On that tour, tragically, the cargo plane carrying Frampton's and the rest of the band's gear crashed just after takeoff in Venezuela en route to Panama. Left without their gear, including Frampton's prized 1954 Les Paul Custom, which adorned the *Frampton Comes Alive!* album cover (and was later recovered in 2012 through a series of incredible, serendipitous events), the band and management tried to cobble together enough gear to continue with the Panama shows but eventually had to cancel. This was met with understandably uncomfortable resistance from the shows' promoter, Manuel Noriega (yes, that Manuel Noriega). However, Frampton and the rest of the team managed to get out of the country and regroup in Miami. Dworkow flew to New York, secured gear for the band, and then returned to San Juan, Puerto Rico, to finish the tour.

"We got back from the tour and were regrouping," Dworkow says. "Peter was recording for A&M Records. It was November, and we were scheduled to start recording after the holidays. We flew out to California to A&M Studios in Hollywood [now Henson Studios]. Peter Frampton had a long history of nontraditional recording environments. He likes to play live, so we arranged to set up the entire band on the Charlie Chaplin Stage [part of A&M Studios and now called the Henson Soundstage], roll in a mobile recording truck, and hit 'record.'"

They went into the studio with Peter, John Regan on bass, and Arthur Stead playing guitar and keyboards, but they still had to flesh out the rest of the band. Producer David Kershenbaum brought in drummer Jeff Porcaro from Toto, and Jeff brought in Steve Lukather.

"We had the first-call studio musicians in the LA recording scene," J. D. continues.

> It was exhilarating, and it added a great energy to the band. But we had the obvious issue that we needed to replace the gear that was destroyed in the plane crash. So I went on a shopping spree.
>
> So here we are, in Los Angeles, and we're starting to make inroads with the recording. I've got to get guitars, amplifiers, and things to inspire Peter to be creative again. As one can imagine, he was really down and disappointed after losing all his creative tools. I talked to the folks at Gibson, Fender, Marshall amplifiers, and we started putting together enough gear so that we could get things rolling. While we were doing this, we also were making new friends with Jeff Porcaro and Steve Lukather, and they, along with the rest of the LA music scene, were having a big influence on Peter.

The album *Breaking All the Rules* (released in 1981) peaked at number forty-three on the US charts and is best known for the title track, co-written by Procol Harum's lyricist, Keith Reid. In addition to the album's commercial success, modest by *Frampton Comes Alive!* standards, recording in Los Angeles with the cream of the LA crop opened Frampton's ears to that tight, eighties, guitar-driven, West Coast sound.

"This was 1981," says Dworkow.

Van Halen's first album only was three years old. The Super Strat and Frankenstein guitars, where you take the basic Stratocaster setup and put a humbucker in the bridge [position], was part of the Van Halen revolution in the music business—that attitude where no instrument was sacred in the guitar business. Peter was taken in by this, and Lukather was our connection into that late-seventies / early-eighties music revolution. He played with tremolo. He did divebombs. He was just an inspiring and very supportive collaborator.

Lukather comes from a place where there's an emotional connection to the instruments. It was an eye-opener for Peter. Peter was always very gear-centric and a very competent recording engineer. He's always been eager to learn how different signal-processing gear works. He's just like a sponge. And one of the things that we started talking about was the guitar pickups Lukather was using, a Super Strat–type setup, in his Mike McGuire–built Valley Arts guitars. This was when we were exposed for the first time to EMG pickups.

At that point, beyond getting the gear to record the album, J. D. needed to start preparing for the next tour. He and Frampton flew up to Santa Rosa and met with Rob and Bill. They also connected with Tatsuo Okada. Fernandes had moved past the Gibson lawsuit era by that time, but their guitars were still as close to copies of Fenders and Gibsons as the law would allow. Fender was still losing the battle between mass production and quality control at the time, and in many people's opinions, the Japanese models were actually superior. Frampton had Fernandes build him a Strat-style guitar with a locking nut, tremolo, and three EMG SA pickups.

Dworkow shares the following:

On the tour that we that we did in South America, Peter had a late-fifties, red, maple-neck Stratocaster that he played "Show Me the Way" on. That was his Strat. So we put together a plan for Fernandes to build a Strat replacement. It was a gorgeous fiesta red with a Floyd Rose tremolo. It was the next evolution of that original design. And, of course, it had EMGs.

That became the go-to Strat. We also had a couple of Telecasters that weren't on the tour. We set them up with a single-coil in the bridge and a humbucker in the neck. Those were the first EMG Teles that we had. We also built a doubleneck Strat–style guitar to replace one that was lost in the crash. It had two six-string necks, one in standard tuning, the other in open *G*.

Not to be lumped into the negative connotations connected to the lawsuit-era Japanese guitars, Dworkow took the Fernandes sticker off the headstock and replaced it with one that said "Ventures." This was in homage to heavyweight instrumental giants like the Ventures and Hank Marvin, who not only influenced Frampton significantly but also made the Stratocaster the dream guitar for a generation of young English musicians.

Frampton validated Rob, Bill, and EMG. While many other players used the pickups, Frampton was the first true rock star to actively endorse the product. Soon the brothers found themselves with far more demand for their product than they could possibly keep up with.

It wasn't only musicians who saw the potential with EMG. The music business started to take notice, and regardless of whether they realized it then, Rob and Bill were on the verge of becoming an international company to be reckoned with. Of course, they couldn't do it on their own. At the time it was all they could do to keep up with orders, and it's tough to see the big picture when you're buried under a mountain of circuit boards and soldering irons.

Help came in the form of an energetic, stylish, self-described "people connector" who had already established himself as a key figure in the music-instrument business world. Hap Kuffner and the Turner brothers were already well acquainted. They moved in the same circles and Kuffner was a part of the Steinberger Sound company, whose basses already featured EMG pickups.

"One day, kind of out of the blue, Hap called us," Rob says. "He asked, 'Who are you guys?'"

"I said, 'Well, we're a couple of suburban guys who grew up in LA. We make pickups.'"

"He interrupted and said, 'Yes, we all know that part. What's your plan? Do you have a rep? Do you have this? Do you have that?'"

"I said, 'Well, we've got a couple of guys who sort of work with us. And we're . . .'"

"He said, 'Look, I've got this Steinberger thing. Why don't I take on EMG too?'"

"It took a while for us to say yes. We were just a couple of kids from LA, and he was this hip New Yorker dude. That was a part of a world and a type of guy that we were not keyed into at all. It was a bit scary, but Hap made a proposal. He didn't want part of the company. He didn't want to be paid on commission, because he told us that he'd end up making more money in commissions than we would as the owners of the company."

"'I'd end up making too much money,' he said. 'You'll learn to hate me, and I won't have a job anymore. Just put me on a retainer. I'll go to work for you, and we'll grow this thing together.'"

"We thought, 'Why not?' And that's how it all got started."

CHASING TONE—
THE ARTISTS' JOURNEY
PART 2

Joel Landsberg, Chris Pandolfi,
Richard Battaglia & Nate Lopez

There's a science to choosing the right paintbrush for the job. Synthetic bristles don't soak up very much moisture and are best for latex paints. Natural bristles are best for oil-based paint. Then there are the myriad shapes, sizes, handles, and the surfaces being painted—all before personal preference and past experiences come into play. As mentioned earlier, Rob likes to compare pickups to paintbrushes. If the paint is the sound, the brush/pickup captures the sound, and the canvas is the recording or performance, the analogy works perfectly. Both are transfer mechanisms that either add to or get in the way of the artist's vision. And with both, even though there's science at play, in the end, it all comes down to that artist's vision and whether the tool will take them there.

This next group of artists reflects that relationship between science, sound, and gut instinct. Rob is never one to shy away from a challenge, and this group pushed him to find solutions that were outside of the box. Some required entirely new boxes. Acoustic instruments, extended-range guitars, boundary-pushing music—all made for challenges that pushed Rob and EMG forward.

One of the things that resonated with me most while putting together this section was how often the sonic needs of all players, regardless of musical style, are almost identical. Whether pop, rock, metal, jazz, country, or bluegrass, the nearly unanimous ask is for a clear, honest representation of the instrument. I also like how these players represent such diverse musical styles and tastes—proof that low-impedance humbucking pickups can find a home in any venue and on any stage. It's all in the hands of the players.

JOEL LANDSBERG

"I play acoustic bass guitar," says North Carolina bassist Joel Landsberg, "which is one of the real rare birds in the acoustic music world." When Landsberg says "acoustic bass guitar," he's not talking about the classical upright acoustic bass. He's talking about his Ribbecke Halfling bass acoustic guitar. Since 1972, Tom Ribbecke has been known for crafting high-end acoustic archtop guitars. The Halfling bass grew out of a relationship with Bobby Vega and the search for an acoustic instrument that combined the best of both a flat and an arched top. It has a standard jazz-type arch on the treble side, giving it a traditional jazz sound in the higher registers, and a significantly flattened profile on the bass side, providing for a much richer bass response and more sustain. It's truly the best of both worlds—an acoustic bass with tone that can cut through a thick jazz or bluegrass mix while offering a full, foundational bottom end.

Landsberg provides that cutting yet full, foundational bottom in a trio with Swiss brothers Jens and Uwe Kruger. Having grown up in New York, immersed in a melting pot of music and musical styles, Landsberg moved to Switzerland in 1989 and toured across Europe with a variety of country, rock, and jazz groups. During his travels he met Jens (banjo) and Uwe (guitar). In 1995 they joined forces under the name Kruger Brothers, and in 2002, they relocated to Wilkesboro, North Carolina, to be closer to the home of country and bluegrass music.

In the beginning their music focused mainly on bluegrass and Appalachian styles. However, their classical European roots were never far away. In recent years they've embraced that classical heritage even more strongly, playing with classical groups like the Kontras Quartet and various symphony orchestras. Their music melds cultures, traditions, and backgrounds—traditional American roots music meets old-world classical forms. Helping Landsberg find his tone on an already complex instrument in an already complex musical situation played right into Rob's love for a challenge.

"I've worked very closely with Rob to try to come up with a couple of different variations on pickups to go with my sound," Landsberg continues.

"He's been instrumental in helping me over the years—probably the better part of the last fifteen years or so."

Joel met Rob at a NAMM (National Association of Music Merchants) show where the Kruger Brothers were performing. "We immediately developed a friendship," he says.

> Rob loved the way that we were doing things. And of course, he was very interested in trying to help us amplify our acoustic instruments. At the time, I had a fully electric Yamaha TRB5, but I never was really crazy about the way it sounded. I approached Rob and said, "Could you maybe do something for me with this?"
>
> He ended up building me a custom-designed set of pickups for that bass. He had to—literally—do a one-off custom build because Yamaha had a proprietary-style pickup that wouldn't match anything.

Around the same time, Landsberg connected with both Tom Ribbecke and Bobby Vega and began his relationship with the Halfling bass. Landsberg goes on to say,

> In the best of circumstances, amplifying acoustic bass frequencies is a tricky beast. You end up with resonance problems. I had feedback issues and things like that, which made it very complicated to amplify the instrument. When you're playing in a small venue, where you don't have to have a lot of amplification, it's not that hard. But the bass itself is not like a big double bass. It doesn't move enough air. You can't play just acoustically as you would an acoustic guitar. It has to be amplified. Of course, we also play huge outdoor festivals, so I had to have something that could also work on a big festival stage.
>
> I approached Rob with that. I was looking to get more of a natural acoustic sound from the bass. It's a five-string with a low *B*. That was a challenge too. He developed a couple of different prototype pickups for me to try, and we went back and forth until we found one that worked. And he actually did a couple of different styles of the pickup, one alnico and one ceramic. He would send them both to me, I let him know what I liked and what I didn't, and eventually, we got it. Originally, Tom had the pickup mounted on two little rails that came out from the bottom of the fingerboard. It was too close to the neck for me and not quite the sweet spot for the sound I wanted. We ended up modifying it so that it comes off the pickguard, almost where a P Bass pickup would be. The only thing that I did was to put a little rolled-up piece of piano felt under the tailpiece to help some of the vibrations, and that was it. We had it.

Rob is always a lot of fun to work with because he is like a little kid. You know, he's so enthusiastic about trying to help the musician define and create and develop his sound. He's a great guy. We love him like a brother.

CHRIS PANDOLFI

Grammy Award-winning banjo player Chris Pandolfi says,

It's very clear to me that nobody is going to get rich designing and selling banjo pickups. I recognized from very early on that Rob is in it for the pursuit of great sound. And, you know, it really, really makes an impact when you sense that someone cares about the same thing that you care about. You invest so much time learning to play and taking it to the stage. Then you find people like Rob who care and are invested on that same level solely because they love it. Those are the people that I am trying to team up with in my career. It's just been a cool connection. I look forward to keeping on it with Rob and hopefully getting this thing sounding even better and better.

In 2018 the Infamous Stringdusters' album *Laws of Gravity*, with Andy Hall on Dobro, guitarist Andy Falco, Jeremy Garrett on fiddle, double bassist Travis Book, and Chris Pandolfi playing banjo, won the Grammy Award for the Best Bluegrass Album. Pandolfi, Hall, and former guitarist Chris Eldridge met as students at the Berklee College of Music. Pandolfi was the first person to list banjo as his principal instrument at the world-renowned Boston music school. In 2004 the trio headed down to Nashville, where they set out to tap into the roots of bluegrass and, in 2007, released their first full-length album, *Fork in the Road*.

Pandolfi came from a musical family. In 1942 his grandparents founded the Connecticut Opera Association. Chris's grandmother started him on his musical path, insisting that her grandchildren take piano lessons as soon as they were old enough. Music resonated with young Chris, but he traded the piano for a banjo in 1997 and never looked back.

While banjo may be steeped in tradition, one Chris is both firmly rooted in and loves, he's not afraid to take the banjo into uncharted, eclectic territory. Among his solo projects, his Trad Plus is a self-described "banjo-centric exploration of a different sonic world, combining vinyl samples, drums, synths, strings, beats and much more." He's both a purist and a Renaissance man—exploring new music and pushing the instrument's limits while, at the same time, remaining a faithful advocate of the banjo's role in American music.

Rob had experimented with acoustic guitar pickups for years and was inspired to expand EMG into other acoustic instrument realms. The banjo, with its significant unamplified volume, resonance, tone ring, drum-like head, and crystal-clear acoustic tone is arguably one of the most challenging acoustic instruments to amplify well. Its head provides a specific challenge, as it acts much like a microphone diaphragm and picks up other sounds onstage.

In small venues players can effectively place a microphone in front of the instrument and get a solid sound. That doesn't work as well in the larger venues and festivals that the Infamous Stringdusters call home, never mind Trad Plus's need for amplification and signal processing. While there have been many attempts over the years to create an electric pickup to capture the banjo's sound, pretty much without exception, those attempts have missed the mark. Designing an electric pickup for the banjo seemed like a custom-made challenge for Rob, and obviously, Pandolfi proved to be the custom-made collaborator.

"One of the first times we met was at IBMA [International Bluegrass Music Association conference]," Chris says. "Rob gave me an initial version of his pickup. I talked to him a few months later, and he asked me how it sounded. I was frank with him. I told him that I didn't think it sounded that great."

Instead of ending the relationship right there, that dose of reality sparked the fire, and yet another challenge was thrown down. The first version of Rob's pickup design didn't have a rich or full enough tone for Pandolfi. He also couldn't get enough gain out of the pickup without getting feedback from the instrument's vibrating head.

"I told him what I needed," continues Chris, "[was] something that's got a bigger, fuller tone, and is less prone to feedback. It was one big kind of info dump. He came back with the ACB barrel design."

Trying to make a magnetic pickup sound identical to the unamplified acoustic instrument is an impossible task and a recipe for failure. Rather, the approach was to start by capturing those acoustic qualities and adding a stability and directness. Rob achieved both goals by placing a small steel shim under the center bridge post, which took care of the feedback issues. Further, the magnetic pickup then sensed the shim's movement as it vibrated and produced the electric signal. This hit the mark for Pandolfi while wearing both his traditional Stringdusters and his Trad Plus hats. He explains the following:

> When you're playing acoustic instruments in a small, pristine listening environment, you can have it just be about the acoustic, natural tone. But when you're playing in a room that is full of energy and people who are making noise—which is our preferred environment—it really makes it a challenge to amplify the acoustic instruments. I think if you're accepting of the fact that it's a different thing altogether, then it must become more than just trying to replicate that acoustic tone. Of course, you still want it to sound like a banjo, but the way that you get there in that listening environment is not just a simple path of replicating that acoustic sound. You have to jump through some hoops. And that's where the pickup technology comes in. The pickup has got to have good gain before feedback, and then there's the tone. It's got to have that tone. I'm a big tone guy. I'm a big pre-war banjo guy. I've got a bunch of banjos that I own that are all 1930s Gibsons. I want the tone to sound right, and I put a lot of energy into getting that tone. I spend hours in my recording studio with our sound engineer using an analyzer, showing us the differences between what a mic is hearing and what the pickup is hearing.
>
> The banjo is so dependent on clear, clean articulation. You've [got] two things going on. You've got the tone of the instrument, and then you've got the note separation, and if either one of those is not there, then you're really starting to sacrifice the power that instrument has to move people. I love that element of the banjo. On the bluegrass side of things—all those metronomic notes cranking out—it's like you're playing two instruments at one time. That's sort of how I explained it to my students. It's like you're playing the melody of a song, and then you're playing all these notes that surround the melody and still fill out the sound. When you're starting to play fast tempos— you know, 130, 140 beats per minute and up—and you're playing four notes per beat, that's hundreds and hundreds of notes a minute. If people don't have the opportunity to perceive those individual notes, then you're losing something. The challenge for the pickup in the live environment is to get all that dialed in because that's what the instrument is, especially when played in a bluegrass style, and I'm definitely playing it in a bluegrass style. Even though the songs and the production have a much more modern sensibility, the way that I play the instrument is directly descendant of Earl Scruggs. And

so you've got to have that note separation. That's what makes the music have [an] impact on the listener.

Bluegrass guys, myself included, are so drawn to good tone. I work a lot as a producer and I believe, of course, that a great song can inspire someone, really evoke a response, but a beautiful sound can do exactly the same thing. And I'm really drawn to that side of the acoustic instruments. Just one beautiful note played by the right player can elicit such a powerful response.

Rob and Chris's relationship is not over. Plans to push the ACB Barrel concept even further were put on hold as the world paused for the COVID-19 pandemic. At the time of this book's writing, Pandolfi was in the midst of going through pages of notes from their previous experiments and conversations with plans to reconnect with Rob and see just where they can take this sonic exploration of this traditional acoustic instrument with future-leaning musical directions.

RICHARD BATTAGLIA

The route between builder and artist isn't always a direct one. When that stop along the way is a four-time Grammy-winning sound engineer like Richard Battaglia, it can make for a pretty interesting trip. Battaglia's tone journey began in 1976, when he started working for the progressive bluegrass group New Grass Revival. Traditional in their roots and progressive in their appearance, politics, and song selection (covering pop tunes by the Beatles, Bob Marley, and Jerry Lee Lewis, to name a few), while they may have alienated bluegrass purists, the NGR introduced bluegrass music to a new generation of fans. Ironically, the group often provided an entry point for young fans to discover some of bluegrass's founding fathers, like Bill Monroe, Earl Scruggs, and Doc Watson.

After a short-lived breakup in 1981, the group re-formed with twenty-three-year-old phenom Béla Fleck taking over banjo duties. Fleck had already made a name for himself in traditional acoustic music circles with his 1979 debut solo album, *Crossing the Tracks*. His debut would be named the best overall album by *Frets* magazine. By then Battaglia had worked his way through the New Grass ranks, serving as both the band's tour manager and front-of-house sound engineer.

"The band was an acoustic bluegrass band that was playing rock and roll tunes," Battaglia says. "They were just getting started combining microphones and pickups. Trying to do live, loud music with just microphones is pretty impossible, especially back then with the quality of sound systems and the technology. So I came into that, and it was always a battle to get what I considered the necessary blend of the mic and the pickup in order to actually achieve a pleasing sound. It had to do with monitors, pickups in the monitors, the microphones in the monitors—that kind of stuff. So everybody was always chasing a better pickup sound."

Adding to the challenge is a natural, almost unanimous aversion to electric pickups by hardcore acoustic players. Contact pickups and piezoelectric pickups as well as magnetic guitar pickups were used, but they couldn't capture an authentic enough sound for even the most liberal-minded of the acoustic purists. As venue sizes grew, however, finding a way to electrically amplify acoustic instruments simply had to happen.

New Grass Revival played their final show on New Year's Eve 1989, opening for the Grateful Dead at the Oakland-Alameda County Coliseum Arena. Three months after that show, Béla Fleck officially turned his attention toward his even more genre-bending band, Béla Fleck and the Flecktones. Battaglia continued his connection with Fleck, a connection that continues to this day.

The Flecktones originally formed for a one-off gig in 1988 on the PBS-TV program *The Lonesome Pines Specials*. The group—with Victor Wooten on bass, his brother Roy "Futureman" Wooten playing electronic percussion, Howard Levy playing harmonica and keyboards, and Fleck on banjo—took off like a rocket. Their first album, *Béla Fleck and the Flecktones*, was nominated for the Best Contemporary Jazz Album of 1989. The band would receive several Grammys, including those shared with Battaglia for his engineering contributions: *Outbound* (2000), *The Hidden Land* (2006), and *Jingle All the Way* (2008). Battaglia would also share the Best Folk Album Grammy in 2015 with Fleck and his wife, Abigail Washburn, herself a virtuoso clawhammer-style banjoist, for engineering their self-titled debut album, *Béla Fleck and Abigail Washburn*.

The connection that began the work towards a pickup specifically for the acoustic banjo happened in 2010. Rob was at a Flecktones gig at the Wells Fargo Center for the Arts (now called the Luther Burbank Center) in Santa

Rosa, California. Flecktones bassist Victor Wooten was already a longtime EMG player, and Béla's Deering Crossfire electric banjo sported an 81. According to Battaglia, Rob connected with Fleck at the show with hopes of enlisting his services and getting feedback on acoustic pickup prototypes.

"If I remember correctly," Battaglia says, "His first attempt was kind of dismal, and Béla just wasn't into it." But the connection had been made, and the tone-chasing journey was underway.

"Over the years, we started working on stuff together," he continues.

Rob would bring us something and we'd try it out. Béla would do his commentary. It took a bunch of years because Béla always had a lot of different projects that he did, as well as the Flecktones. We really started getting into checking out the pickups when Béla was playing with his wife, Abigail. They had nine banjos onstage. Abby is a clawhammer player and Béla is a Scruggs-style player, two different combinations of styles, which are really great together. They've really made something of that combination.

So we had all these banjos to try to amplify. We had a mic in front of them, and then each banjo had a pickup. We ran through preamps and all that stuff. So it was always challenging to get a good blend of the two of them.

We were still trying to get as close to what his banjo naturally sounds like as possible, but he's not a typical banjo player. His sound is usually kind of fat and warm. It's not a twang kind of thing. He loves to play jazz, and he's always going for that fat, warm sound. The highs are still there, the distinction is there, but it's not missing all that low end. We would rely on the pickup for the lower end and the microphone for the brighter acoustic sound. That combination really works in a live situation. It was warm and mellow, and it doesn't sound electric.

Battaglia sees himself as the go-between for the artist and the builder—Rob and Béla in this case—at least at the start of the project. Once the project starts getting some traction, he tends to get out of the way and let the two parties communicate directly. He's never far from the process, however, and has a more-than-vested interest in making sure that the instruments hit the mark both sonically and practically. With nine different banjos on Washburn's and Fleck's stage being played interchangeably, the tone balance Rob was able to provide was invaluable.

Although it took years, due more to an overload of projects in both camps than a lack of will or desire, from a sonic standpoint, they hit the mark pretty quickly. Only three or four actual pickup prototypes went back and forth. The rest was fine-tuning the details, and that work is still ongoing (at the time of this writing). Battaglia shares the following about the process:

> Little by little, we're getting closer and closer to something that Béla is satisfied with. We're there, sound-wise; it's more the physicality of it, the size or the way the volume knob works, things like that. Rob has just stuck with it and kept coming back. All the little things that we did ask for, Rob would just come back and say, "Here, try this. I've done this for you." And things got better and better. For example, when the pickup is mounted on the banjo rim, Béla hits the volume control every once in a while, and so the volume changes on him. Of course, he doesn't want that, so we asked for an indent or something like that, so that you can set the volume at a point, and it wouldn't move very easily.
>
> I've been lucky enough to work with all these guys who are so impeccable about what they do. They know what they want and if they're happy with what they're hearing. I know what their instruments sound like, and I know what they're going for in a live situation. Most of the time is just trying to get there—which is a joy. I couldn't ask for anything more.

They were getting really close to working out all those minute yet critically important details when, first, massive Northern California forest fires occurred, and then COVID-19 got in the way. Battaglia is confident that they'll get to the end of the journey (and will likely have by the time this book is published).

NATE LOPEZ

Sometimes it's all about being in the right place at the right time. It also helps if you're an exceptional player, playing great, funky, jazz tunes on a custom-made, extended-range guitar that covers the roles of a bass and a guitar in one instrument.

Nate Lopez was playing a solo gig in Sebastopol, California, just seven miles away from EMG headquarters. Chrys Johnson was handling EMG's A&R at the time and was at the gig. Johnson connected with Lopez after his set and said, "We love what you're doing. We have this really cool arch-top jazz pickup, but we don't have any artists on our roster that play it. Would you like to come down and do some videos for us? You can play whatever you want, your original tunes, your own arrangements, whatever you want. We'll record them and put them out on EMGtv [the company's YouTube channel]."

Needless to say, Lopez jumped at the opportunity, and a great relationship was born.

Inspired by the old-school jazz guitarists like Joe Pass and Kenny Burrell and heavily influenced by today's crop of solo funky guitarists led by fellow multiscale guitarist Charlie Hunter, Nate transitioned from piano to a standard acoustic guitar through bass and, finally, to his current, custom-made eight-string guitar with three bass strings, tuned E, A, and D, and five guitar strings, tuned A, D, G, B, and E.

"I grew up in a musical family," Lopez says.

My mom made me play piano. I started taking lessons when I was really young, but I never really enjoyed the piano, because you couldn't bend notes. My dad was listening to Santana, B. B. King, stuff like that, and I couldn't emulate that on the piano. So I became frustrated with it and quit.

My uncle was a fantastic guitarist. He wasn't famous, but he played folk music and was pretty well known locally. He would play whenever the family got together. He did tapping and all kinds of really neat stuff, which was pretty unusual for a folk guitarist in the seventies and eighties.

Unfortunately, when I was thirteen or fourteen, he passed away. My dad ended up with his guitar, and he gave the guitar to me to play around on. I really enjoyed messing around with that old acoustic. After a month or two, I realized I was pretty much just playing bass lines—old Creedence Clearwater Revival bass lines, anything like that, anything funky, Pink Floyd, Black Sabbath, that kind of stuff too.

Before long Nate had transitioned to bass full-time and was playing in local Latin and jazz bands. As his musical knowledge, skills, and palette grew, he was drawn to classical guitar, not only for the sound but also for the repertoire and the ability to play multiple parts on one instrument. He began studying with friend and teacher Matt Grosso and later studied at the Ali Akbar College of Music in San Rafael, California. From Grosso, Lopez learned classical technique and chord voicings, and he applied those to his five-string bass. He tuned the two lowest strings to E and A, like on a standard four-string bass, and the higher three strings to *G*, *C*, and *F*, which moved him into the guitar range.

"I had higher chords and stuff like that," he says. "I figured I had enough bass notes with just the two lower strings. I did that for a while, and then a friend of mine turned me on to Charlie Hunter. That was everything that I'd been looking for. I went I went to see him at Yoshi's [Nightclub] in Oakland, and it really blew my mind. I understood exactly what he was doing. His technique and everything that he was doing made a lot of sense to me. This was the answer."

Since his debut on the Disposable Heroes of Hiphoprisy's critically acclaimed album *Hypocrisy Is the Greatest Luxury*, featuring the tune "Television, the Drug of the Nation," Charlie Hunter has been at the head of the new breed of jazz/funk guitarists. In 1993 he released his first solo album, *Charlie Hunter Trio*, and set a standard for the soulful, groove-based, funk genre that he not only helped to define but in which he continues to raise the bar to this day.

Though he plays guitars with several different setups, the guitar Hunter is most identified with—the one that put the pieces together for Lopez as well—is an eight-string Novax custom instrument made by West Coast luthier Ralph Novak. According to the Novax website, "This unique instrument allows you to drive the rhythm section with solid, deep bass while comping or soloing rich guitar riffs at the same time." Tuned *E*, *A*, *D* (lowest three strings of a bass), *A*, *D*, *G*, *B*, and *E* (highest five strings of a guitar) with separate pickups and outputs for each string set, the instrument truly sounds like a bass and guitar played at the same time. Each string grouping can be sent to separate amps or effects, making the distinction between the two voices even more pronounced. According to Novak and those who play his instruments, the element that truly makes the instrument work is his patented (now expired) Fanned Fret design. This Fanned Fret, or multi-scale, design allows for the scale length of each string to be individually set to optimize both the pitch and string gauge. String tension and harmonic response are enhanced, making the extended-range guitars like Hunter's more sonically balanced and better sounding.

Lopez would eventually get a Novax, but first, he had a custom seven-string guitar made for him by fellow Sonoma County resident Michael Dolan. He played that instrument for a couple of years before making the jump to a Charlie Hunter model eight-string Novax. Shortly after getting that instrument, EMG entered the picture.

The pickup that EMG needed to be demonstrated was the Ron Escheté–inspired 91. In typical arch-top jazz guitar style, the pickup floats above the instrument's top and attaches either to the neck or pickguard. Lopez went to the EMGtv studio and ended up recording tunes on several different instruments with different pickup combinations, including the 91 on a Tacoma archtop and a seven-string headless Strandberg. After the shoot, Johnson told Lopez to bring a few guitars over to the shop, and he'd put some EMGs in them. Lopez first brought an ES-335 copy.

"I didn't know all the model numbers," says Lopez.

I just told him that I really like that semi-rolled-off tone, that T-Bone Walker kind of really warm sound with a little bit of grit and a little bit of that old forties or fifties amp distortion. They set me up with a couple different pickups, and they nailed it. It was fantastic. I thought, "Okay, great. Let's put something like this in my Novax."

When I put the EMGs in my Novax, all my gear lit up. My pedals sounded so much more distinct. My amp sounded cleaner. I was able to get the kind of gain tones from my amp that I had always heard in my head. I was just really blown away by those EMGs, how bright and clear and articulate they made my gear sound. I was sold at that point and started gigging with that Novax exclusively.

I played that for a while and really enjoyed it, but I had always liked the hollowbody sound of my 335, and I wanted my own instrument. I eventually ended up finding LHT guitars and Tyler Wells. Tyler actually came to me and said, "I see you play these fanned-fret guitars. I've got a six-string with a one-inch fan. Why don't you check it out and tell me what you think?"

Playing the LHT guitar for the first time was amazing. He loaned me one of his six-strings, and I was just blown away by the attention to detail all across the board. At this point, I had a pretty good idea what I wanted: hollowbody, semi-hollow at least; headless; and fanned frets. I went to Tyler and said, "Can you make me an eight-string hybrid headless guitar?" And his first response was, "No way! I build arch-top guitars, and they're fancy and multiscale, but they've got headstocks."

Lopez and Wells went back and forth, eventually landing on the NL-8 signature model: a headless, multiscale, hollowbody headless guitar. When it came to pickups, there was no other option than EMG. Lopez shares more:

> I loved the pickups in my Novax. I said to Tyler, "Let's just call up EMG and put the same things in there." When we called, Rob said, "Oh, you're having this custom instrument completely designed and made? Let's make you a custom pickup. I'll wind it myself. We'll make you a custom three-string bass pickup and a custom five-string guitar pickup." I wasn't going to say no to that!
>
> Rob based it on the P60s that were in my Novax. I said, "Okay, well, this is an instrument that can't have any crosstalk, but I want you to put the pickups right next to each other—oh, and also fanned frets. He didn't even blink; he was just excited about it. He just jumped on it and started drawing up schematics.

They went back and forth a couple of times to get the spacing right, but before too long, they had it nailed down. LHT has since made a travel-friendly version of the NL-8, the "Funkstick," with the same pickups.

Living in Santa Rosa has only strengthened Lopez's connection to the EMG company, as well as making it easy for him to stop by for repairs or tweaks.

"Just being able to go to EMG and have Bobby Vega sitting there in his little cubicle with his little mini stack, playing," continues Nate, "just being so open to showing you things and saying, 'Hey, check this little thing out!'— they're more friends than business partners. They're very approachable and just really easy to do business with—always cool."

5

WELCOME TO THE BIG LEAGUES

***Art Thompson* (Guitar Player, *January 2000*):** *Are you still playing the Cloud guitar?*

Prince: *Yeah, but it's painted blue now.*

AT: *Who built that guitar?*

P: *It was made by David Rusan.*

AT: *Do some instruments have a more spiritual vibe than others?*

P: *I'm spiritual by nature, and I appreciate the time it took someone to make an instrument. It doesn't matter if it's a guitar or a synthesizer, someone still had to take the time to make it.*

***Dave Rusan* (to the author, *July 27, 2020*):** *There weren't a lot of specific things Prince asked for, but he wanted EMGs. He never talked about the stuff you would think you'd talk about in custom guitar conversation—neck size, fret sizes, you know. He had a bass with some of the features he liked, and he just said, "Make a guitar like this." He wanted the EMGs, though. It wasn't me who picked those out. He wanted it white with gold hardware, spade-shaped markers. That was about it.*

If you listen to his playing, there's a lot of clarity. The EMGs hold up under a lot of overdrive. They get a definition that you wouldn't get out of an overwound, high-impedance pickup. He must have liked them because I made two more for him to tour with. I made the one for the movie [Purple Rain], which you know was a playable guitar, but I had thought of it kind of as a movie prop. When they requested two more, I thought, "Oh well, Jeez. I guess he really wants to play the guitar live too." I hadn't really thought ahead like that. Although, if the movie had been a flop, there wouldn't have been a tour to go with it, I suppose. But the film was a success, and he wanted the same thing, so I started whipping up more.

Jim Reilly: *Did you change anything from the movie guitar for the others you built?*

DR: *No, he still used the SA and the 81. He used them on recordings and live all the time. The guitars stayed with him right until the end, through many repaintings. In the end he had other people make them, too, because he wore mine out, but he kept with the EMGs.*

(Note: *In June 2020 Prince's Cloud guitar no. 2 sold at auction for $563,000. Three years earlier, a teal blue version sold for $700,000.)*

It was a perfect rock-and-roll moment. The young, struggling prodigy walks his beautiful girlfriend past the music store and looks longingly at his dream guitar in the window. The girlfriend takes note, sneaks back, and buys the mythical instrument. She gifts it to him, and just when all seems lost, the guitar god in the making channels the cosmos and creates a sonic masterpiece with the gift from his muse. Even though this was a scene from a movie—Prince's seminal eighties rock film, *Purple Rain*—the iconic image of the musician finding the perfect instrument to tap into that unnamable musical source holds true.

In the beginning EMGs found their way onto players' instruments through repair shops. The clear, loud, low-impedance signal with no degradation over long cable lengths solved many guitarists' problems. Carruthers, McGuire, and others who were the industry's go-to fixers never kept EMG a secret, but their influence never reached the average guitar or bass player. For that, Rob and Bill needed a sales team—enter Hap Kuffner.

Kuffner has been a fixture in the music business since 1969, when he and partner Stan Jay founded one of the first dedicated vintage stringed-instrument stores, Mandolin Brothers, in Staten Island, New York. As

Mandolin Brothers and the vintage guitar market took off in the seventies, Kuffner branched out beyond musical instrument retail. He figured that the real money was to be made in manufacturing and wholesale. Through a series of chance meetings—first, at the 1979 NAMM show and then, later, at Mandolin Brothers—Hap connected with Ned Steinberger, who had a radical new bass design that needed a company to bring it to life. Steinberger, Kuffner, Jay, and technical consultant P. Robert (Bob) Young founded Steinberger Sound in 1980. Jay handled business and promotion, Young provided invaluable technical support, Hap was the sales guy, and Ned was the visionary. That vision included employing EMG pickups.

"They were the only pickups Ned felt were going to be good for Steinberger," Kuffner says. For a couple of years, Steinberger offered other pickup options. "They sounded good," continues Kuffner, "but the low-impedance preamp EMG sound was what guys wanted."

Rob and Bill Turner first saw Ned Steinberger's headless bass design at the 1979 Summer NAMM show in Atlanta, Georgia. Steinberger had a small space in the La Bella Strings booth and was showing the music community his headless carbon-fiber bass guitars for the first time. He was still in the prototyping phase. However, with their radical, minimalist design, the Steinberger basses weren't attracting too much attention. Rob was intrigued by the design but remembers thinking that Steinberger would need to start his own company to both make and market his instruments, foreshadowing what was to come a couple of years later with the creation of the Steinberger Sound company.

As Steinberger Sound found its footing and started developing their headless basses in earnest, Ned turned to EMG pickups. "I saw an ad in a guitar magazine for EMG pickups," says Steinberger. "They were promoting a new, advanced technology, which didn't mean a whole lot to me initially until I learned more about it. I was trying to create a new and exciting instrument. They were creating a new technology. I thought I'd better check into the latest technology in pickups. Why wouldn't I? I called and got some pickups from Rob, and we went from there."

The first commercially available Steinberger basses offered a choice of either another company's high-impedance pickups or low-impedance EMGs. Overwhelmingly, customers preferred the EMGs, and within a year or so of regular Steinberger bass production, they dropped the high-impedance option. Ned's molded carbon-fiber Steinberger basses had very clean output with very even harmonic response. Combining that natural sound of the instrument with the hi-fi, quiet, clean, active EMGs was a combination that could cut through the most complex band situations.

Rob created a unique pickup for Ned's basses. When listening to the instruments' unamplified sound, he felt like they lacked midrange. So he added steel to a ceramic magnet and crafted a split-coil, Precision Bass–style humbucker that he then placed into a regular guitar-sized humbucker housing. The Steinberger Sound L2 bass loaded with two EMG SS (Steinberger Sound—today, renamed the HBCS) pickups, voiced specifically for Steinberger, came to define the progressive, bass-forward eighties pop and rock sound. The bass cut through the mix and played a huge role in moving the instrument from the back of the stage to the forefront. The instrument's sound was a combination of Ned's design, the headless system's stability, carbon-graphite fiber's stiffness, and Rob's electronics.

Steinberger became the first company to use EMG as their original equipment manufacturer (OEM) supplier. Steinberger guitars with EMG 81s, 85s, and SAs soon followed and were equally as sought after as the basses. One needed to look no further than Steinberger's success to find proof that EMG had arrived.

Kuffner's connection with EMG would soon expand far beyond his role with Steinberger sound. He shares the following:

In 1982, Ned went to visit with Rob and Bill. At that point, they were still working out of their small garage in Santa Rosa. When Ned returned, he said, "Boy, those guys could definitely use some marketing or sales help."

I called them, talked to Rob, and he invited me out. I went to Santa Rosa and met with them. Rob took me through the whole story—how Rob is the drummer, Bill the guitar player. How they took apart vintage humbuckers and changed the magnets, doing the dirty work, all of that stuff. How Rob had figured out that if you added a preamp onto a pickup and sent the signal to a preamp on an amplifier, you could do low-impedance signal. Rob told me about his dad, who put a soldering iron in his hand when he was just a kid and said, "Here, learn this."

I was interested in the company and working with them and said, "Okay, what are you doing in New York?"

Rob replied, "Well, we've got a sales rep." And he told me the rep's name.

I said, "Well, that's interesting. That sales rep is also the sales rep for a different, rival pickup manufacturer. That's not going to work."

We worked out an arrangement. My first task was to head back to New York and politely tell their old sales rep that I was replacing him. We were friendly competitors, so it wasn't that big of a problem.

Hap's second task was to head out to 48th Street, New York City's music row. Steve Friedman, who had opened a guitar shop right across the street from the vintage store (called We Buy Guitars) of his dad, Larry Freidman, immediately signed on as a New York retailer. Hap also connected luthier Stuart Spector to Rob and Bill. Between Spector and Steinberger, the EMG bass sound heavily influenced eighties pop. Still, Kuffner was far from done.

"Rob had never liked the NAMM shows," Kuffner says. "He told me that they had done several, and nobody had really paid them any attention. I said, 'Okay. Let's go to Frankfurt.'"

The Frankfurt Musikmesse held its first annual trade show in 1980 [in Frankfurt, Germany]. From the beginning it rivaled the American NAMM show in terms of influence, especially throughout Europe. Hap had already taken Steinberger instruments to the show and found success in a European market eager to embrace new North American sounds. Rob was game, and in 1983, he and his soon-to-be wife, Karen, headed overseas with Hap.

"At that point, we had maybe six different distributors selling Steinbergers in different countries in Europe," Hap says. "They were already doing Steinbergers, and when we showed them the different EMG pickups and how you could put the engine of the Steinberger into a P Bass or Jazz Bass—or any other bass—they signed up."

Bernhard Kurzke first met Hap at the 1981 Musikmesse. His retail shop, No. 1 Musik Park in Hamburg, was one of the hubs for musicians looking for both European and North American instruments. However, even if most weren't quite ready for the sight of the headless Steinberger basses loaded with two active EMG pickups in 1981, the sound was undeniable.

Kurzke shares the following:

As we were walking to our exhibit area, we passed by a little space, four-by-four meters, no curtains, just the back walls. There was a single table and a chair. In the middle, this guy was sitting, playing a headless bass. We'd never seen a headless bass before. He'd play it, then he'd bang it on the floor, pick it up, and continue playing to show that it stayed in tune.

We went to our booth, and a little while later, that same guy showed up. It was Hap, and he asked us, "Do you have a ladder?" That was the first sentence he ever said to us. He was smashing down the Steinberger bass, and he hit the footrest he was using. The footrest flew up and got stuck between two walls. I went over to his booth with our ladder, went up, and got his footrest. That was our introduction to Steinberger.

We had all these guys coming from Hamburg to the show, and I told everyone to go to that booth and close their eyes. Don't look at the instrument. Just listen to it. It sounds great. They came back and said, "Yes, it's a fantastic instrument."

From that auspicious beginning, Kurzke became the first European Steinberger distributor. A couple of years later, when Hap showed up representing both Spector Basses and EMG, Kurzke jumped without hesitation. He was already an EMG fan.

In 1981 guitarist Don Dokken showed up at No.1 Musik Park. He needed money to fly back to the States and offered up his Charvel Super Strat–style guitar (two single-coils and a humbucker—all active EMGs). "He opened the case," Kurzke says, "and there was this guitar. It had flames on the body. We had never seen anything like it before. We couldn't even figure out the brand name at first because it was in such small print. We figured out that it was 'Charvel,' and my salesman said that Don was a friend, so we bought the guitar from him. It sounded incredible. The next day I phoned Grover Jackson [owner of Charvel Guitars at the time], flew over to Los Angeles to meet with him, and became Charvel's first international distributor."

He also knew about low-impedance signals and the benefits of active guitar systems. In addition to Charvel, Bernhard's company distributed a system called Power Pots. This was an external box the guitar plugged into so as to boost the signal and create a low-impedance signal.

"But Rob was taking it one step further," Kurzke says, "by putting the electronics into the pickup housing. When EMG became available, I thought, 'Fantastic, this is precisely what I was looking for.'"

He continues, "We introduced them first to the Netherlands and then to other countries in Europe. In the very beginning, we sold them only to musicians and then added dealers. Bass players were the first to buy them because of the Steinberger influence."

European guitarists took a little longer to jump on board. "We did well with the Charvel guitars," Kurzke says, "but beyond that, EMGs on guitars were rare. When Valley Arts came out with their artist series and the Lukather model, that's when things took off."

The relationship between EMG and Kurzke has continued on and off since the early eighties. "Rob is inspiring," Bernhard continues. "He has his own good ideas, and he and his brother Bill were a great team. Most importantly, they're reliable. They're honest. You can talk to them. You could speak with them right from the start. You can talk to Rob, give him something to consider, and he'll make a decision you can rely on. That's the best thing I can say about a business partner."

For Rob, Bill, and the other half-dozen EMG employees, those days were all about production. Back orders took two to three months to fill. Out of necessity, all their energy focused on production. With a flourishing international sales team, more work than they could handle, and all signs pointing towards more business ahead, the team needed help to keep all the pieces from overwhelming them.

Gary Rush and Rob had been friends since they were kids in Long Beach. They played drums together, shared the same taste in music, and had similar world views. Rush had been drafted and spent a couple of years in Vietnam. Rob narrowly avoided the draft. He had actually drawn a low number in the draft lottery, which meant that he would undoubtedly be called. However, Rob's year of eligibility was 1973, and before his number could be called, the then president Nixon ended conscription. Gary was a year older than Rob and had his number called the previous year. The two never lost contact, though. Gary wrote letters regularly, and they stayed connected throughout Rob's adventures up the West Coast and as EMG took off in Santa Rosa. After his service, Rush returned to Los Angeles but was stuck in a dead-end job delivering Sparkletts bottled water.

"Gary was a very smart, intelligent guy," Rob says.

> We were talking about how I needed someone to help with the management end of things and immediately realized that he was the perfect person for the job.
>
> He said, "Okay, I can come work for you, but you're the boss. Don't say yes or no to something just because we're friends." It worked. He was very influential in a lot of the decision making. He was conservative with money

and had a real calming influence on our growth. Although he says he worked for me, he really worked with me and pretty much took over running the business side of things.

Gary took care of the inventory and managed the supplies, staff, and payroll. Bill and Rob worked primarily on the production and training new employees. And the company exploded. In 1982 EMG had a staff of fifteen. By the end of 1983, they had doubled that and doubled again to over sixty by 1985. They had moved from the garage into a Quonset hut building and kept adding more and more. They had taken over five huts and still needed more space, so they moved again. This time they set up shop in an industrial park, where they took over five thousand square feet of a commercial building, which they shared with a welding company. By 1985, they had taken over the entire space, all ten thousand square feet. EMG eventually bought the building and personalized it to meet their needs.

"Those days were really all about sales and production," Rob continues. "It was going to NAMM shows, working with Hap, hiring reps, increasing production. Luckily, we had a team of people—Gary, especially. He put in a tremendous amount of work. Gary was one of those people who would work twenty-four hours a day. He was single and poured all his energy into his work. And there was a tremendous amount of work, just keeping us on the straight and narrow."

As the eighties established itself through style, fashion, and music, so too did EMG. They had Steinberger on the East Coast, Valley Arts on the West, a solid foundation in Asia, and a foothold in Europe. Soon the big boys came calling. Interest in active electronics was heating up, and Fender wanted a piece of the action.

At the time, Fender was struggling. Sales were down. Competition was at an all-time high, and in many people's opinions, their instruments' quality couldn't compete with smaller builders like Valley Arts and the considerable number of Asian competitors. On top of all that, fashion had worked its way into the mix like never before and was now firmly a mandatory requirement for musical success. MTV, which premiered in August 1981, had ushered in a new era, and for young bands trying to catch a fickle audience's eye, the traditional Stratocasters and Telecasters didn't cut it.

In an effort to right the ship, CBS, Fender's parent company, recruited three of Yamaha's senior executives: John McLaren, William Schultz, and Dan Smith. They were tasked with reinventing Fender's reputation, stopping the monetary bleeding, and attracting the young guitar and bass players who saw Strats and Teles as their fathers' guitars.

Fender's first experiments with active electronics came in 1980 with the Fender Precision Special bass. The bass was built with a traditional Precision Bass body with a split single pickup. While the pickup itself was passive, they added a nine-volt battery-powered preamp to the bass's electronics, producing a low-impedance signal. The preamp could be bypassed and the bass played in passive mode, offering the choice of a wide variety of sonic options. Visually, the instrument lived up to its "special" branding. Fender first offered either candy apple red or Lake Placid blue finishes with a matching-colored headstock and the choice of a rosewood or maple fingerboard. Later they added an Arctic white finish option, as well as a natural walnut body. Gold-plated hardware, a brass bridge, and white pickups and pickguard (black on the walnut version) were standard on all Precision Specials. By all accounts, the basses were a little on the heavy side but sounded great. The Specials were only in production through 1982 and in very limited numbers. In 1983 they were replaced by the Fender Elites.

"In 1982 Fender approached us," says Rob.

> They wanted to make a series of guitars, designed by a couple of guys who used to work for Peavey. [The design team included Dan Smith, Chip Todd, John Page, Charlie Gressett, and Freddie Tavares.] They came to us and said, "Hey, we want you to make some pickups for these instruments. We want to show them off in three different studios: Cherokee, in LA, which was basically the home of the Beach Boys; a studio in New York; and another one in Nashville. They were all excited and gung ho.
>
> They made up some housings for us that looked the way they wanted them to, and they put the Fender logo on them. John Page came up to the factory. We were still in those Quonset huts, and we had about six or eight employees. We built our pickups into their housings. We put an SA pickup in the Strat. We did a Tele that had two new pickup designs—those actually became the EMG 60s. It was a mini-humbucker with ceramic magnets, as opposed to alnico in a narrow mini-humbucker-size housing. We did a P Bass with our standard P Bass–style pickup, what we call the original recipe. We also did a

Jazz Bass. The Jazz Bass had side-by-side coils, as opposed to one long, single coil. It had this sort of beefy tone, not totally different from a typical Jazz Bass but thicker and fuller.

They installed our stuff on maybe half-a-dozen guitars. Then they took them away. We didn't hear anything from them for a couple of months. All of a sudden, they called, all excited again, and said, "Okay, you need to come down here, and we need to talk."

Bill and I went down to Fender headquarters in Fullerton [California]. We were put in an office. I have to preface this by saying that we were naïve, to say the least. Here we were at Fender, and we had a factory with only eight people. They started throwing out big numbers of pickup orders. "Bring it on," we said, "as much as you want. We can tool the housings. We can do it all. It'll be ready in about ninety days. Bring it on."

Well, they weren't having it. They said, "Okay, look, boys, you're not going to be able to make enough stuff for us. If this thing takes off, we're going to build around three thousand instruments a month, which means we're going to need nine thousand pickups. We're going to need a lot of stuff from you guys, and you're not capable." We thought we were capable, and we went back and forth for a while. In the end they said, "Well, we don't think you are, but we want to buy your company."

"Wow," we thought. "This is interesting. Fine. How much are you offering?"

"Five thousand dollars," they said. Five grand!

This is the part that absolutely blows my mind, especially in retrospect. Here are these design guys, along with John Page, putting this thing together. They've gone to all these studios. The guys in the studios are all really loving it. The producers are saying, "This P Bass sounds better than any P Bass I've ever heard. Don't ever bring another bass in here." And they offered us five grand?

We basically just said, "Well, we don't think five grand will cut it; that's not going to happen." They asked us how much we wanted for the company, but we weren't for sale. That wasn't the plan. Truthfully, even if they had offered fifty or a hundred thousand, we weren't for sale. We told them that if they wanted our product that we were going to have to make it for them, and we walked away.

In the end the Fender Elite Stratocasters, Telecasters, and P Basses took off from where the Precision Special left off, with a battery-powered preamp between the pickup and other electronics. The pickup and preamp were designed by Paul Gagon, who went on to become the vice president of technology at BBE Sound Inc. Production only lasted for two years, 1983–1984, and were sold in retail stores until 1985. Reviews for the Elites at the time were much like the Specials—great-sounding, solid, and heavy. Unfortunately, the Elite Stratocaster's tremolo system did not garner rave reviews and led to an overall negative impression in the marketplace. Today both the Specials and the Elites hold a unique place in Fender history and are sought by collectors and players alike.

In hindsight, Rob dodged a bullet by avoiding selling his company and giving his product over to an industry giant. Even though they were tiny by comparison, they were already making giant inroads into the sonic landscape, and those roads would only become more and more traveled.

For Rob, Gary, and the rest of the EMG team, the dream was coming together. The lessons Rob learned while winding coils and soldering his dad's radios were paying off in spades. He had listened when his dad told him that one needed a product of one's own to be successful. No one could have imagined how significant and influential Rob's product would become. For the first time since hanging out the EMG shingle, Rob and Bill were making enough money to do more than just pay the bills.

On a personal level, life was coming together for Rob as well. Karen Elizabeth Johnson started working for Neils Chew at Dowling Miner Magnetics in 1978. Dowling Miner produced industrial, educational, and toy magnets. The company was close by, in Marin County, and an obvious choice to supply EMG.

"It was a just a small shop at the time, with just me and Neils working in the office," says Karen. "I got to know Rob because I would call him for money. Every once in a while, he would come into the shop to pick up magnets, and we would chat."

This went on for a few years until, finally, in 1981, Neils—likely sensing an attraction between the two (pardon the obvious magnetic pun)—encouraged Rob to ask Karen out for a date.

"So he asked, and we went out," continues Karen. "Our first date was at this little restaurant in Novato [California] at the Hilltop Restaurant, and we had a great time together. I thought everything was great, but then I didn't hear from him. I was just starting to wonder if I had blown it, and then on Thursday night, he called me and said, 'Hey, you want to hang out this weekend?' I said, 'Sure, why not?' And that was that. That's what happened every week. I wouldn't hear from him until Thursday night, and then he would call me up. Since the very first time we started dating, we would see each other every single weekend."

It didn't take long for Rob to move out of his brother's house and move in with Karen. She was living with a friend, and her friend's boyfriend was eager to move out of that situation. With Rob in Santa Rosa and Karen in Marin, they decided to meet halfway in Petaluma and have been there ever since.

On October 8, 1983, they married. For their honeymoon they had booked a room in the Ahwahnee Hotel in the Yosemite National Park. The Ahwahnee Hotel is best known as the visual inspiration for Stanley Kubrick's film *The Shining*. They never made it to the hotel, however, opting to spend their honeymoon representing EMG at a tradeshow in Japan.

"We stopped in Hawaii on the way back," Karen adds. "So it wasn't all bad."

On March 3, 1988, they welcomed their first child, a son they named Matthew. A little over a year later, on November 30, 1989, daughter Alison joined the family.

While the pieces were all falling into place both personally and professionally for Rob, those same pieces were starting to fall apart for brother Bill. Shortly after Rob moved out of his brother's and moved in with Karen, Bill and Patty's marriage fell apart. Drinking and a little pot had always been around but were only ever used recreationally and didn't impact the work or their personal lives. However, as Bill's home life strained and cracked, harder drugs—notably, cocaine—became more and more present. In the summer of 1983, Bill jumped into the rock-and-roll lifestyle with both feet, and it would soon overtake him.

"We did all the guitars for the ZZ Top *Eliminator* Tour," says Rob. "Their tech brought in their guitars, we installed all the pickups, and Bill left to join them on tour. He wasn't there for the whole tour, maybe only a dozen shows or so, but he came back a mess. That was really just fuel to the fire. He wasn't in great shape before he went on the road, but that pushed him over the edge."

From that point on, Bill's commitment to EMG slowly and steadily declined. Where it was once Rob and Bill, increasingly Rob took over as the head and heart of the company. Bill would leave EMG officially in 1989, but according to Rob, since about 1985, he was there only in spirit. Their stories couldn't be any more different. On the one hand, you have Rob pushing EMG further with new designs and an ever-increasing roster of superstar players. On the other, you have Bill drifting away. Bill's story doesn't end with EMG. He continued to add his voice to the guitar landscape after leaving EMG. (That voice is explored in chapter 7.)

Steinberger basses and guitars; Spector basses; custom shops around the world; dedicated reps in North America, Europe, and Japan; and the cream-of-the-guitar-tech crop all played their role in solidifying EMG's place in the eighties musical landscape. But the most significant sonic force, the one to take EMG over the top, was building strength and about to explode in a feast of auditory fury. Studio players loved the sound, clarity, and presence of EMG pickups. Live, you could color the sound with a wall of effects and not lose any of that transparency. A new musical power was brewing, conveniently for EMG, in and around the San Francisco Bay Area. All the qualities that made EMG the choice for Steve Lukather, David Gilmour, Prince, Leland Sklar, and so forth were precisely the same qualities that the fast, aggressive, loud, wall-of-sound metal bands needed to make their voice heard. Once unleashed, that voice simply could not be silenced.

EMG PLAYERS LIST AS OF JUNE 1, 1985

Carlos Alomar
Bill Laswell
Mark Andes / HEART
Geddy Lee / RUSH
Michael Antony / VAN HALEN
Sara Lee / GANG OF FOUR
Fernando Von Arb / KROKUS
Will Lee

Richard Bannister
Phil Lesh / THE GRATEFUL
DEAD
Joc Bartley / FIREFALL
Kerry Livgren / KANSAS
Steve Lukather / TOTO
Garry Gary Beers / INXS
Graham Maby / JOE JACKSON

Christopher Bishop
Eddie Martinez
Jack Bruce
Mark Mendoza / TWISTED
SISTER
Bobby Caldwell
Wendy Melvoin / THE
REVOLUTION
Erik Cartwright
Ronnie Montrose
Jerry Casale / DEVO
Tom Morrongiello
Mark Chatfield / BOB SEGER
BAND
Jamie West-Oram / FIXX
Phil Chen
Ben Orr / THE CARS
Bill Church / SAMMY HAGAR
BAND
Jerry Peek / STEVE MORSE
BAND
Stanley Clarke
Mike Peters / THE ALARM
Phil Collen /DEF LEPPARD
Guy Perry / THE MOTELS
Jeff Cook / ALABAMA
Gary Pihl / SAMMY HAGAR
BAND
Joe "King" Corasco
Jeff Pilson / DOKKEN
Buck Dharma / BLUE OYSTER
CULT
Tiran Porter
John Entwhistle
Ron Escheté

Steve Rodby
Earl Falconer/ UB40
Niles Rodgers
Dan Fogelberg
Carmine Rojas
Robben Ford
Fernando Saunders
Lee Fox / SCANDAL
Robbie Shakespeare / BLACK
UHURU
Peter Frampton
Gene Simmons / KISS
Billy Gibbons / ZZ TOP
John Simpson / THE SOS BAND
Kirk Hammett / METALLICA
Leland Sklar
Steve Harris / IRON MAIDEN
Scott Smith / LOVERBOY
Colin Hay / MEN AT WORK
Mark St. John
Dusty Hill / ZZ TOP
Paul Stanley / KISS
Wolf Hoffman / ACCEPT
Roger Steen / THE TUBES
Ron Jennings
Sting / THE POLICE
Alphonso Johnson
Jamaaladeen Tacuma
Brothers Johnson
Garry Tallent
Percy Jones
Pat Thrall
Darryl Jones / MILES DAVIS
Richard Thompson
Mat Thorr / ROUGH CUT

Danny Klein / J. GEILS BAND
Vinnie Vincent
Bruce Kulick
Scott Thurston / THE MOTELS
Stevie Ray Vaughn

Bob Weir / THE GRATEFUL
  DEAD
Andy West
Bill Wyman / THE ROLLING
  STONES
Vinnie Zummo

6

ENTER SANDMAN

Jim Reilly: *Take me back to those early days of the San Francisco Bay Area thrash metal scene. What was the attraction to EMGs?*

Tommy Armstrong-Leavitt: *The EMGs didn't lie. You couldn't hide behind anything. They kept you more honest than other pickups would. It's like with a really great condenser mic—you can hear a pin drop in the background. With another mic, you wouldn't notice that. So you're going to hear everything. If you suck, you suck, but at least you're going to hear it.*

They were big and powerful, and when you put it in rock and roll, it was like using this clean, killer microphone. It just didn't have the noise or the extra hiss or squish. It was very immediate. The immediacy of the attack changed the way some players would approach their playing. Guys that got used to it never left it.

There were some who didn't like it being so immediate. It's like if you're driving a car and you have brand-new brakes, you feel it right away. It's like, boom, you're stopped. If you have older, worn-out brakes, just before the stop, you're going to have to pump them just to get it to slow down. That's like an old-school, passive, alnico 2 pickup. But an active pickup stops dead, like brand-new brakes. It just works that quick.

CHAPTER 6

JR: That analogy also speaks to how the sound of the pickup itself led to the music and how the new music demanded that pickup. It's a symbiotic relationship between the two.

TAL: Well, you know, the fact of the matter is that if there's a band breaking ground in a particular genre, and other bands are in that genre, they're all going to be asking, "What do they use? We're going to use that, too." You have bands like Metallica to blame for that. Their first record wasn't EMGs. On Ride the Lightning, *I think Kirk had started using EMGs. But by the time they got to the third record,* Master of Puppets, *that was all MESA/Boogie amps and EMG pickups.*

As early as 1980, a new musical wrecking train was gathering steam in and around the San Francisco Bay Area. In Los Angeles the DIY punk ethos was being replaced by hair metal bands like Mötley Crüe and Ratt, but five and a half hours north, that same punk energy was feeding a new brand of music that skipped glam for intensity and fury. Fueled by the virtuosity of hard rock bands like Rush, Led Zeppelin, and Iron Maiden and infused with punk rock's energy and power, a new crop of angry young kids was forging a musical genre that was too punk for hard rock and too hard rock for the punks.

This music was fast, intense, and heavy—a new outlet for teenage angst. Distortion with saturated tone was a must, and palm-muted guitar lines added an intentionally unnerving percussive assault. Synchronized unison lines that played at breakneck speed, snare drums and double kick drum lines that shot out like machine-gun fire, and vocals that were no less intense and cutting all called for instruments that could deliver a clear, crisp slap to the face. On the guitars and basses, EMGs were the perfect fit. With no lack of irony, the same features that made EMGs work so well for the commercially conscious LA studio players less than a decade earlier were precisely the same qualities that made them work so well for these antiestablishment Bay Area metal bands. Like all good revolutions, this one evolved over time, and before the rest of the world had even realized that it had begun, it was already a force to be reckoned with.

Exodus was one of the first bands creating the scene; it was formed in late 1979, when high school classmates Kirk Hammett, Tim Agnello, Tom Hunting, and Keith Stewart connected over their shared love of seventies hard rock and the new wave of British heavy metal bands like Iron Maiden, Motörhead, Black Sabbath, and Judas Priest. Soon they were playing around San Francisco and adding originals to their metal-heavy covers. After a handful of personnel changes, in 1981, guitarist Tim Agnello was replaced by Exodus roadie Gary Holt. Holt quickly became the band's primary songwriter and driving force.

Exodus wasn't the only heavy band on the San Francisco thrash scene. Death Angel, Lääz Rockit, Possessed, Blind Illusion, Metal Allegiance, Vio-lence, and others pushed the boundaries with loud, intense, angry, often-violent music. And while players were searching for the tools to make these new sounds, EMG's prominence in the Bay Area made them an easily found option to modify and hot-rod guitars. Add that to the fact that many of the bands influencing this new musical crop—Kiss, Judas Priest, and the Scorpions—had already found EMG pickups, and soon active 81s, 60s, and SAs become the signature sound for many thrash metal bands. The music's power couldn't be contained to Northern California. Bands across North America and around the world jumped on board, with Anthrax, Metallica, Megadeth, and Slayer emerging as the "Big Four" bands who defined the genre.

Before the scene even really became a scene, an expanding group of like-minded kids converged around two poles. One was Ron Quintana's Rampage Radio show on the University of San Francisco's radio station, KUSF. Every Saturday night from 1:00 a.m. to 3:00 a.m., Quintana played the heaviest metal of the day. He opened a young Kirk Hammett's ears and those of his broadening group of hard rock-loving friends to the big players, like Motörhead, Saxon, Scorpions, Judas Priest, Iron Maiden, and lesser-known bands like Trust, Raven, Venom, and Accept.

The other touchstone, the live music venue of choice, quickly became the Old Waldorf Hotel at 444 Battery Street and their Metal Mondays. Jeffrey Pollack opened the Waldorf in 1976. In 1980 he sold it to legendary concert promoter Bill Graham. The club served as a beacon for both up-and-coming local and established bands doing the West Coast club circuit. Among others, AC/DC, Dire Straits, Blue Öyster Cult, Blondie, REM, and U2 all played the six-hundred-person-capacity room, as did a young band in the early eighties who hadn't yet relocated to the Bay Area from Los Angeles: Metallica.

Kirk Hammett's guitar journey started at age fifteen. He explains,

> When I first started playing guitar, I had a realization that I liked loud, fast, aggressive music with power chords and riffs, big drumbeats, and dynamic arrangements—just searching my way through the types of music out there and what type of music really appealed to me. That's the music that hit me the deepest. It was hard rock, you know, the beginnings of heavy metal. Bands in the seventies like Deep Purple, Black Sabbath, Led Zeppelin—they were called heavy metal, but it was really more like blues-based hard rock. Looking back, what really defined heavy metal was yet to come.
>
> And so, for me, I liked those bands and other bands that I still listen to, like Aerosmith, Thin Lizzy, Kiss, the first Montrose album. Then the first Van Halen album came out, and that guitar sound was incredible. I love that first Van Halen album. I spent so much time sitting down with it, learning, learning so much of it. But the entire time, I just knew that on my rating system, it was only maybe six and a half out of the ten on my own personal meter of heaviness. Then one day, I heard UFO. A friend brought over a UFO album. We put it on, and I heard Michael Schenker's guitar sound, which was Gibson Flying V straight into a Marshall amp.

At the time, inspired like so many others by Jimi Hendrix, Hammett was playing a Strat. With Eddie Van Halen playing a Stratocaster-style guitar with a humbucking pickup, the first Van Halen album prompted Hammett and, once again, many others to put humbuckers into their Strats. That hot-rodded Strat sound was close, but hearing UFO and Schenker playing his Flying V straight into a cranked Marshall stack blew the doors off. After hearing the results of when a friend had put humbuckers into a Gibson SG copy, Hammett decided that the only way to get the sound he was after was to get his own Flying V and Marshall.

"I eventually got my Flying V," he continues.

> I traded my Strat, did various jobs, worked at Burger King, and then, eventually, I got a Marshall half-stack too. I was set. I had humbuckers through a Marshall, but it still wasn't quite there. And all of a sudden, you know, I was hearing stuff like Judas Priest and Iron Maiden and their guitar sounds, which were more gained-out. And, I thought, "What am I going to do? I'm not getting *that* sound."

It was in about 1981, while still in Exodus, before I joined Metallica—I was a guitar freak, a guitar nerd. I still am. I buy every single guitar magazine that comes out. I have done that ever since I started playing guitar. So I saw, I think it was in a *Guitar Player* magazine, a little ad in the corner. It was a small ad, an illustration, not even a photograph, and it said, "EMG Pickups, Active Pickups, get more output, battery-operated pickups," you know, the whole spiel. I looked at this and thought, "Wow, what a great idea!" It was the first time I'd seen a guitar pickup that was supplemented with outside voltage, you know, with a battery. I didn't know if there were any other pickups out there that did that, but that caught my eye. It made sense to me immediately, you know, higher gain, higher output, output equals higher gain, but you know, this was 1981, and I had no disposable income.

Hammett's financial situation didn't change overnight. Still, it did take a significant step in the right direction in 1983 when he got a call from Metallica, who had temporarily set up shop in New York and were about to begin recording their first full-length studio album, *Kill 'Em All*. Conflicts were common and intense between then lead guitarist Dave Mustaine and the rest of the band. Once in the studio and heading down a pretty promising road, those conflicts proved too much, and Mustaine was fired.

Metallica and Exodus were well acquainted with each other. They moved in the same San Francisco metal circles, listened to the same bands, and even shared stages, including gigs at the Old Waldorf. Kirk even recalls being a part of a group of friends who held a "goodbye and good luck" party for Metallica as they headed off to the East Coast to make their first major jump toward the big leagues. On April 1, 1983, the then lead guitarless band called Hammett and asked if he'd be interested in trying out for the vacant position. Kirk jumped on a plane (it was his first time leaving California), met up with the band, played the tune "Seek and Destroy," and the rest is history.

Kill 'Em All came out to early critical acclaim. It would go on to sell over three million copies worldwide. While it wasn't an overnight success, it did garner a devoutly loyal and rapidly growing group of fans. Metallica hit the road with James Hetfield on guitar and vocals, drummer Lars Ulrich, Cliff Burton on bass, and Hammett firmly holding down lead guitar duties.

"So *Kill 'Em All* comes out," continues Kirk, "and we go on tour."

At that point, someone put a PAF pickup, a real Gibson Patent Applied For pickup, into my Flying V. So for that one tour, I had a PAF pickup in there and used that all the way up until just before we left to record *Ride The Lightning* [Metallica's second album, produced by Flemming Rasmussen and recorded in Copenhagen, Denmark].

Somehow or another, I'd gotten enough money to buy one EMG pickup. I put it in my V, and instantly my sound was so much better through the Marshall. We did the entire *Ride the Lightning* tour with the EMG pickup in my Flying V. I also had EMG pickups in the Edna guitar [a 1983 Fernandes Stratocaster–style guitar] that's on the cover of the *Garage Days* EP. I remember on the *Ride the Lightning* tour, guitar players coming up to me, going, "How are you getting that sound out of a Strat?" They were so amazed, and I told them I had EMG pickups, and they were like, "What's that?"

I used those guitars for the entire *Ride the Lightning* tour, and they were fucking great. Then we signed with Elektra, we got an advance, and we're about to go to Europe to record *Master of Puppets*. I took that advance, got another EMG pickup for my V and a MESA/Boogie amp. With that MESA/Boogie amp and two EMGs in my Flying V, the sound was right there. Both James and I had gotten MESA/Boogie amps, and I told James that he had to try EMG pickups. We fell in love with that sound and have never stopped using them. Once we got our ESP endorsement, whenever we ordered a guitar, they would naturally come with EMGs.

Hetfield's path to EMGs reflects many other players' journeys toward a tone of their own. The band had been together since 1981, when Hetfield answered a musicians-wanted ad in the Los Angeles *Recycler*, placed by drummer Lars Ulrich. Originally, Ron McGoveny played bass, and Dave Mustaine covered lead guitar duties. The band hit the LA scene but felt no kinship with the emerging hair metal scene. Their cassette demo, *No Life 'Til Leather*, and subsequent shows drew some significant attention in San Francisco, though. They fit right in with those early heavy bands and the emerging metal scene. The other draw in San Francisco was bassist Cliff Burton. The band coveted Burton, and when he agreed to join them as long as they relocated to San Francisco, the group, sans McGovney, needed little more convincing. Once established in San Francisco, Cliff Burton replaced McGovney on bass, and in 1983, once Hammett left Exodus and replaced Mustaine on guitar, the classic Metallica lineup was set. (Mustaine and bassist Dave Ellison would go on to form another giant thrash metal band—Megadeth.) As Metallica's success grew, so did Hetfield's understanding of how to get the sound he needed to fuel the music and inspire both him and the band. He shares the following:

> Right from the start, we were very competitive and wanting to improve our sound. We heard all of the Van Halen wannabe bands down in LA and the Ratts and stuff like that. Their sound was super saturated, but they weren't really punchy or clean.
>
> After we moved up to the Bay Area, when we first got going and were getting a little more recognition, more love for what we were doing, everyone was really in search of a very percussive, crunchy sound. I was, for sure. It all kind of happened at the same time—ESP guitars, MESA/Boogie was up here, and then EMG all connected at the same time. It kind of was this perfect storm of three things coming together. When I first tried EMG pickups, it was as if someone made a pickup especially for me and my sound that I'd been searching for. It was fat, it was crunchy, but it was still clear and percussive. And that was what was important to us.

Hetfield settled on an 81 in the bridge position for distorted rhythm and a 60 in the neck for clean lines. Metallica's growth went hand in hand with Hetfield's understanding of those factors that create and influence tone. An expanding bank account didn't hurt the search either. On his first guitars, whatever stock pickup the instrument came with was good enough.

"They weren't even real Gibsons," he says.

> They were copies. I didn't think much about pickups at all. I just thought, "Well, whatever the guitar sounded like, it sounded like, and it was all about the amplifier." But then, as the world opened up for us, we started learning more. We were very into our sound and learning more about it. Being in the studio, being more involved, being more a part of the production, you realize how every little thing makes your sound what it is.
>
> The healthy competition in the Bay Area was a big factor in pursuing that tone, pursuing the ultimate sound. For me, it was as if the drums and guitar were attached; that's what it would sound like—that percussive attack. Clean picking stuff was very important too. I've always loved playing clean guitar. Those contrasts are a big part of our sound. And to me, the 81 and the 60 were like the two most extreme pickups. The 60 and 81 combo was just perfect.
>
> Certain guitars, certain amps, certain pickups, make you play differently. What I really loved about the 81 is the saturation and thickness of it. I mute

so much, and I barely have to touch it, and it would do its thing. That would allow me to play faster. So I got a little more adventurous with my playing. My sound lived in this 81, and I could put it in any guitar. I could take whatever guitar and put it in there and know that I was 80 percent there with my sound.

In many ways thrash metal's explosion mirrors that of EMG. Metallica and EMG grew up together. While musicians, builders, and producers may have known about active pickups' benefits and the secret to the sound of studio players like Lukather and Sklar, as Kirk Hammett, James Hetfield, Gary Holt, Frank Bello, and others became a generation's guitar and bass heroes, players of all levels were swapping out stock pickups for EMGs. They wanted to sound like their heroes, and for many, EMG was one of the pieces that got them closer. EMG's role in creating the sound of Metallica continues and evolves to this day. Hetfield, Hammett, and current bassist Robert Trujillo have all worked with Rob and EMG to create signature sets that have taken the standard pickup combinations to an even more personalized and influential level.

Due in no small part to hard rock and the Metallica-led thrash metal scene, electric guitar sales boomed during the eighties. Rock and metal topped the charts, each band with a prerequisite guitar hero leading the way. Guitar manufacturing had become a global entity with all of the major companies and an overwhelming collection of smaller ones competing for the attention of an abundance of young people trying to become the next Eddie Van Halen.

Through Hap, Rob met Jack Westheimer. In 1959 Westheimer became one of the first importers of musical instruments into the United States, first from Mexico and then Japan. In 1973 he partnered with Young H. Park and built a factory in Korea to manufacture mostly inexpensive, entry-level guitars. By 1976 exports from their Korean factory to international markets exceeded those from Japan. As the company grew, in addition to their own brands such as Cortez, Cort, and Kingston, their Korean factory produced instruments for Ibanez, Epiphone, Fender, Squier, Hohner, Alvarez, Kramer, JB Player, Dean Guitars, Lakland, and Hohner, among others.

Westheimer had licensed the Steinberger headless guitar and bass hardware systems and was producing his own budget headless instruments under both the Cort and Hohner brand names. They wanted an inexpensive pickup to go along with their designs and felt they needed the EMG name to add credibility.

"The only problem was that we weren't making an inexpensive pickup," says Rob. "That's when we developed the 'Select: Designed by EMG' line. I designed a complete line of passive pickups—not active but just passive pickups. It was a partnership between Jack, Hap, and me. We called it KTW. Jack did the manufacturing, I did the design, and Hap sold them. It worked out really well, and we made a lot of money very quickly. We did just the four basic pickups: a humbucker, single-coil, P Bass, and Jazz Bass."

While the budget-priced passive Select line wasn't intended to replace or even compete with the active EMGs, they more than filled the need to have a high-quality pickup on an entry-level instrument. The income also played a critical role in ensuring stability and continuing EMG's growth.

"Throughout those years, from 1985 through 1987, we were just growing like mad," says Rob. "We were in a new building. We had changed our production system to a surface-mount process [a technique of mounting components directly on a circuit board], which allowed us to double our production. We brought in a couple of machines, which actually required us to hire more people. We ended up with around thirty people just building circuit boards."

Gordon Barnes joined the team and took over a lot of senior engineering work. As a company, EMG really hit its stride. They added a line of accessory circuits based on the designs they had originally done for Fender and continued refining old models and creating new ones.

"We had stacks and stacks of pickups," Rob continues.

It was incredible. It blows my mind now how much stuff we were making. It seemed like every year we were adding something new. The 85 was done in 1985. The 89 was done in '89. The 89 is still one of my favorite designs. It's actually two pickups in one, a dual-coil and a single-coil, each with its own preamp. It's definitely the ultimate, as far as what you can do for switching.

The main thing was that we were becoming broadly known as both a guitar *and* a bass pickup company. We were filling out and carving a unique place in the market. Those were days when there was a lot of growth, a lot of money, and a lot of changes.

The EMG 89 set the bar for the EMG pickups that followed in terms of both sound and technology. Many other models have expanded upon its flexibility and tone options. More important, it cemented the foundation upon which EMG's place in the music industry would become firmly and unquestionably rooted. In hindsight, the timing could not have been better.

The company's birth, growth, and rise through the marketplace mirrored the growth, boom, and plateau of the larger music business world. As the eighties turned into the nineties, technology entered the picture in ways never before imagined. Vinyl records and tapes had already been supplanted by compact discs, and soon mp3s and new approaches to music distribution, such as Napster, would completely flip the recorded music industry upside down. The Internet began replacing music magazines as the source for information about the latest pieces of gear. Small instrument companies that had found success in the eighties by offering high-quality alternatives to the industry giants like Fender and Gibson found themselves being bought out by those heavyweights. Sometimes, they would continue production under their original names with new bosses pulling the strings. Other times, smaller brands were simply swallowed up and slowly disappeared. After years of steady growth and innovation, Rob looked around and realized that he had reached the top of the mountain.

"It was 1991," he says, "and I'll never forget it. I was at the NAMM show in Anaheim, and I looked around and realized that none of us were growing anymore. The computer age was starting to take off. We could see the internet coming. And, looking four or five years into the future, I'm sure that there were a lot of music retailers who were really starting to wonder if they'd be in business or not."

In the music retail world, this was the beginning of the acquisition era as well. Guitar Center began life in 1959 as the Organ Center, catering mainly to the home and church organ market. By 1964 founder Wayne Mitchell had branched out and, in the following years, became one of the largest sellers of Vox guitars and amplifiers, due in no small part to Beatlemania. They rebranded themselves the Vox Center. In 1971 they were renamed again—this time to Guitar Center—and aimed their sights on the entire rock community. They rode high in the eighties with the focus on guitar-driven rock and, by the mid-nineties, had become the largest music chain in North America.

Similarly, MARS (Music and Recording Superstore) Music set out to create a music retail network of superstores in the mid-nineties. In just a few short years after opening its doors in 1996, former Office Depot president Mark Begelman had created the second-largest music store chain in the United States. Other American companies, like Sam Ash, jumped on the trend towards creating big-box music stores. Around the world the trend continued. In Canada, Long and McQuade was buying up small, mom-and-pop music stores across the country. In Europe, Thomann Music led the way, and in Japan, Shimamura Music became the retail music megastore and one-stop shop for all things musical instrument-related.

For many stores that had opened their doors in the fifties and sixties and had both created and capitalized on the rock-and-roll explosion, these large corporations, along with their deep pockets and buyout offers, provided an exit strategy and retirement plan for their owners. For Rob and many other manufacturers, it meant a narrowing of their customer base and a new set of challenges.

Smaller guitar manufacturing companies were being bought up by larger corporations as well. Steinberger, EMG's first OEM company, had been swallowed up by Gibson. Their second OEM, Spector Bass Guitars, had been bought by Kramer in 1985, and Kramer, too, was taken over by Gibson in 1997. While it may have looked like there were still countless brands represented on the music store walls, an increasingly smaller and smaller number of companies called the shots.

"I first noticed the change at the NAMM shows," Rob says. "Attendance was terrible. People weren't going because you basically had five guys buying for five hundred stores. The business model in the industry had changed. If you didn't have an established brand name, those five guys weren't interested in you." Luckily for Rob and EMG, they were firmly in possession of an established brand name.

"We had a history," he continues. "We had some artists behind us, and we didn't have to launch anything new at that time. Our product was on vinyl."

Being "on vinyl" translates to EMG pickups and the sound of EMG pickups being responsible for countless songs, solos, bass lines, and hits over a changing musical landscape. Musical genres such as Metallica's thrash metal, the LA-session player-inspired pop scene, and the eighties bass-forward new wave were defined by the EMG sound. Their sound was the sound of multiple eras' rock and roll, jazz, country, and pop. As others fell by the wayside, the music retail world narrowed to a handful of key players. In the world of instrument pickups, EMG had become the equivalent of a Fender or a Gibson. They had become an institution, and they weren't leaving.

With that foundation and the security of industry clout, Rob had the freedom to explore new sounds, take on interesting new challenges, and chase tone in the purest and most rewarding sense. The music of high-profile artists, such as Pink Floyd, Prince, Metallica, and Frampton, played with guitars and basses loaded with EMG pickups and solidified EMG's place in the rock music lexicon of the twentieth century, and that level of respect and prestige only paved the way for more products, more pickups, and more music to come.

*Bill and Betty Turner in
Long Beach, mid-1940s.*
Rob Turner personal collection

Dede, Rob, and Bill, early 1960s.
Rob Turner personal collection

Bill Sr.'s Skywatch Pro, the radio receiver that changed everything for the Turners.
Author's Photo

July 15, 1967: The Doors at the Anaheim Convention Center. Rob and Bill were way up in the back.
(Courtesy Anaheim Public Library)
https://bit.ly/3BPJQSq

Rob's 1971 high school senior-year photo.
Rob Turner personal collection

Rob just a few years later, as the music world takes hold.
Rob Turner personal collection

One of the first Dirty Works EMG pickups, circa 1974.
Author's photo

Built by John Carruthers, Lee Sklar's Frankenstein bass. One of the most recorded basses in pop music.
Lee Sklar

Ned Steinberger in 2022 with Tony Levin's 1979 fretless, EMG-equipped Steinberger bass guitar. This instrument was Ned's first Steinberger sale.
Ned Steinberger

The Turner brothers doing business as Overlend at a NAMM show, late 1970s.
Rob Turner personal collection

Rob with Gary Rush.
Rob Turner personal collection

Dave Rusan with the first Prince cloud guitar, made specifically for the film Purple Rain.
Dave Rusan

Rob, Tatsuo Okada, and Bill in Japan, mid-1980s.
Rob Turner personal collection

Karen, Rob, and Hap Kuffner travelling the world for EMG.
Rob Turner personal collection

Nili Brosh and her Ibanez custom shop guitar, with a passive EMG H1A in the bridge position and passive S1s in the middle and neck locations—a classic "Super Strat"-type setup.

Courtesy of Nili Brosh

Nate Lopez with his custom LHT hybrid, multi-scale guitar.
Nate Lopez

Grammy-winning sound engineer Richard Battaglia at work. (Photo Credit: Yu Pei)
Ricard Battaglia

Chris Pandolfi rocking the EMG banjo system.
Chris Pandolfi

Slipknot's Jim Root with custom Daemonum signature pickup set. (Photo Credit: Anthony Scanga)
Courtesy Slipknot

Robert Trujillo with his signature Riptide EMG set. (Photo Credit: Brett Murray.)
Courtesy of Q-Prime (Metallica management)

Trujillo, Hetfield, and Hammett: Riptide, Het Set, Bone Breaker—the Metallica frontline, EMG equipped. (Photo Credit: Jeff Yeager.)
Courtesy of Q-Prime (Metallica management)

James Hetfield putting the Het Set through its paces. (Photo Credit: Jeff Yeager.)
Courtesy of Q-Prime (Metallica management)

Zach Harmon at Metallica head-
quarters with Kirk's 1959 Les Paul
Standard: Greeny.
Zach Harmon

Victor Wooten and one of his Fodera Monarchs, with the EMG PJ setup.
Victor Wooten

Bill's LSR roller nut on a Fender Stratocaster. (Photo Credit: Kelly Leavitt)
From Kelly Leavitt

Bobby Vega, Stu Hamm, and Rob in Vega's bass corner at EMG headquarters.
Rob Turner personal collection

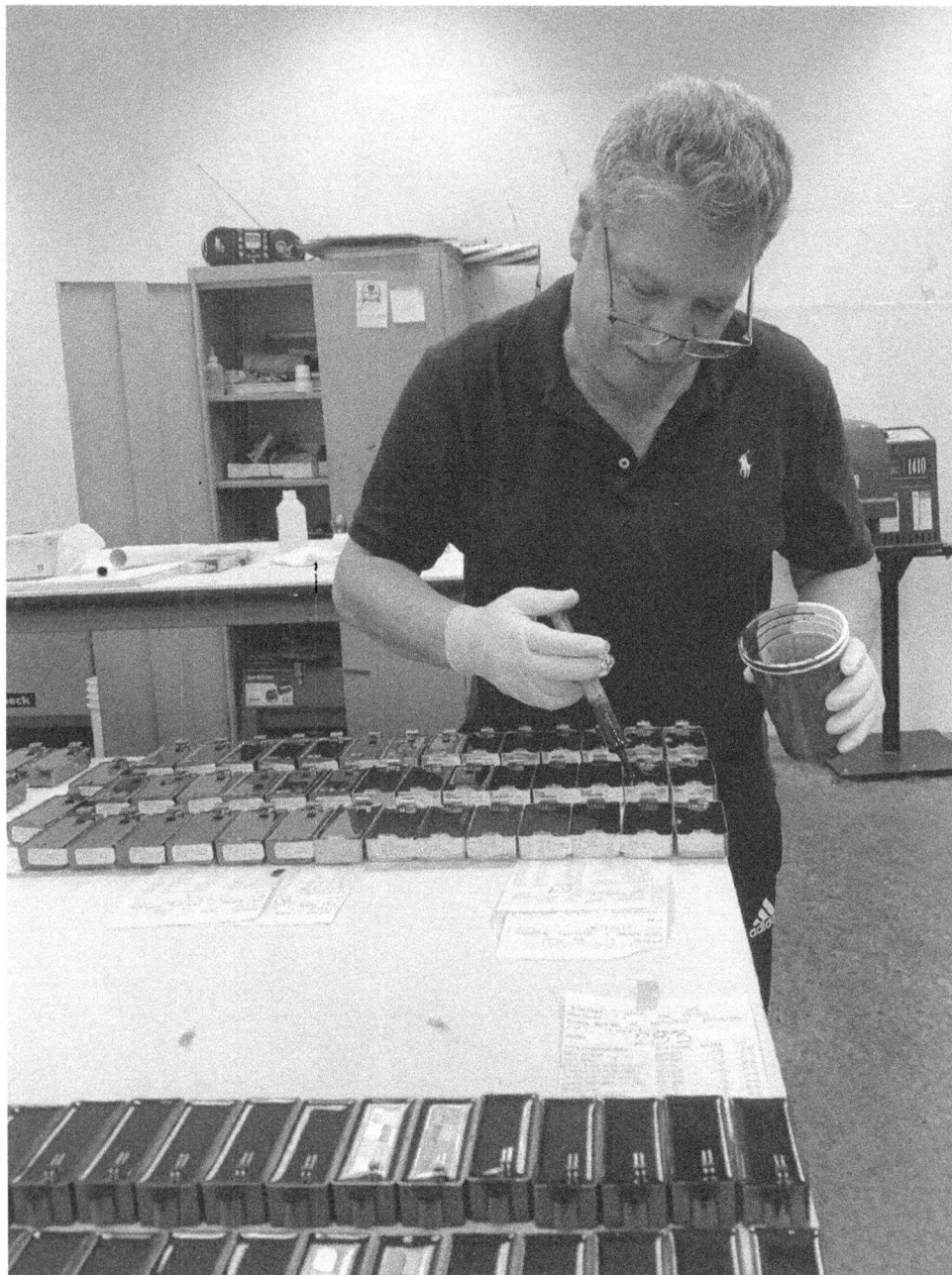

Miguel Hernandez potting EMG humbuckers at EMG headquarters in Santa Rosa, CA. Each pickup is still done by hand.
Author's photo

Attorney Gene Tunney's orders from 1973, still posted on Rob's office wall.
Author's photo

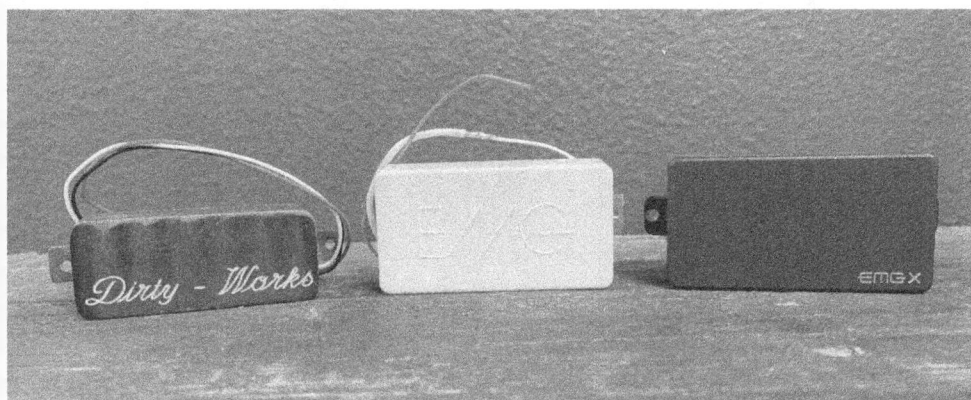

From Dirty Works to Overlend to EMG: the EMG pickup's evolution.
Author's photo

The Turners: Rob, Matt, Alison, and Karen.
Rob Turner personal collection

The author and Rob Turner. Petaluma, CA. May 23, 2022. (Photo Credit: Tom Mulhern.)
Author's photo

CHASING TONE—
THE ARTISTS' JOURNEY
PART 3

Robert Trujillo, Kirk Hammett, James Hetfield (& Zach Harmon)

The tone journey continues. As this section picks up where the last "Chasing Tone" interlude left off, we keep returning to relationships. While these stories reflect shared passions, growth, evolution, and a mindset that never stops exploring, they also involve no small amount of trust—trust in a friend, brother, mentor, or tech to journey down a road with an uncertain destination.

Metallica tech Zach Harmon epitomizes this relationship. He's been a trusted member of the Metallica family since the beginning. The band trusts him explicitly. As the following stories make clear, when he tells Robert Trujillo, Kirk Hammett, or James Hetfield to take note, they listen.

Another particularly revealing story involves British bassist Guy Pratt. At the beginning of the rehearsals for Pink Floyd's *Momentary Lapse of Reason* tour, Pratt mentioned to his tech, Syd Price, that the pickups in his treasured 1964 Fender Jazz Bass were a little quiet and that they should, perhaps, look at replacing them. When he arrived at rehearsals the next day, Price had swapped the instrument's original pickups with an active EMG J set. After shrieks of exclamation as to what he'd done, Pratt plugged it in, loved the sound, and the EMGs have stayed in his bass until this day. Pratt tells the story with a little more color: "I said to my tech, Syd Price, one day, 'These pickups are a bit quiet. Maybe we should think about getting some new ones?' And the next morning, it had EMGs in it. I shouted, 'What the fuck have you done? You can't put EMGs in a '64 Jazz!' But when I plugged it in, it sounded amazing!'"

Once again, these are just a few stories of musicians who found their sound with a little help from Rob and EMG. While EMG has played a role in all of these musicians' growth, in no way are they the only factor—not even close. But they played a role. There's no hidden message that you'll find your sound by swapping out your stock pickups and installing a Het Set. If you do, great. If you don't, keep looking. Maybe that's the message: keep looking, searching, seeking, exploring, changing, evolving, growing, and playing.

ROBERT TRUJILLO

Robert Trujillo grew up in Culver City, California, surrounded by music. His mother filled his ears with Motown, and his dad's tastes ran the gamut from the Rolling Stones and Led Zeppelin to Beethoven. At fifteen, Robert inherited a hollowbody Harmony bass from a friend of his dad's, and a lifelong love of the instrument was born. Over the next few years, skateboarding, surfing, and bass playing fought for his attention. Inspired by bass legend Jaco Pastorius, the bass won out. He played with various friends during his high school years and, before long, was playing Rush, Ozzy Osbourne, and Led Zeppelin covers at backyard parties. At nineteen he enrolled in the Dick Grove School of Music, solidified his chops, and seriously pursued a career as a studio bass player.

His career took off on the concert stage rather than in the studio in 1989, when he replaced bassist Bob Heathcote in the hardcore punk / thrash metal band Suicidal Tendencies. This led to his role in the funk/metal supergroup Infectious Grooves, featuring Trujillo, Suicidal Tendencies's Mike Muir on vocals, guitarists Dean Pleasants and Jim Martin, and drummer Brooks Wackerman. Trujillo's work in Infectious Grooves caught the ear of Ozzy Osbourne, and at thirty-two, the bassist found himself at the top of the hardrock mountain, working with Ozzy from 1996 through 2003.

In 2003 he landed one of the most coveted jobs in rock—the bass spot in Metallica.

Bassist Jason Newsted had left the band two years earlier, kicking off their two-year search for the right person to fit the bill. The band was in no rush, opting to have producer Bob Rock cover the bottom end on the album they were working on, *St. Anger,* rather than risk bringing in the wrong guy. While the list of players who had the chops to fill the void was long, it took the right combination of personality, ability, work ethic, and vision to land the gig. Trujillo checked all the boxes. He had first connected with the band when Suicidal Tendencies opened for Metallica on a 1993–1994 tour. A couple of years later, he'd bonded with Kirk Hammett over their shared passion for surfing. In 2003 when he got the call from Kirk and drummer Lars Ulrich to jam with the band, he was all in. Trujillo's addition and his first days with the band are famously captured in the Metallica documentary, *Some Kind of Monster.* He's been holding down the bottom end in the world's biggest metal band ever since.

Since the very beginning of his professional career, he's been an EMG guy, although he took an indirect and unintended path to that destination.

"I had a bass custom built for me," Trujillo says.

It started out as an Ibanez Musician, but I cut it up and reshaped it to look like a blue [Kubicki] Factor bass. I painted it, added gold hardware, added a tremolo bar. I told this story to Geddy Lee once, and we had a good laugh about it because he had done the same thing to one of his first basses. We both probably should have left them alone because they would have been better in their original state, but I hacked it up to look like another instrument that I admired but couldn't afford.

Long story short, I finally got my bass done and ready to go. I took it to a gig at a club in Venice Beach [California]. I put it down in a corner, might have had a few drinks, and it got stolen. I literally had it just for that day, and it was gone.

A friend of mine, Steve McGrath—he's actually the bass player for Billy Idol now—felt really bad for me. He had just started playing Tobias basses and had a beautiful Tobias five-string. He said, "I'm going to take you down to the shop in Hollywood, on Cahuenga, and we're going to order you a five-string custom. I didn't have a lot of money back then, but I ordered it anyway. I made payments on it over time. After a year, I finally got ownership of this beautiful instrument. It was my first real bass, and I used it in Suicidal Tendencies.

It was Trujillo's friend and fellow bassist Brad Cummings who turned him on to EMG. Cummings was a couple of years older than Robert and a teacher/mentor to Trujillo. Cummings has worked with an A-list of LA projects, including sessions with Sting, Cheryl Crowe, and Dave Koz, to name only a few. These days, in addition to his session work, he leads the Rok Music Academy in Long Beach. Back in 1989, when Brad heard the music Trujillo was playing with Suicidal Tendencies, he told Robert that he had to switch to EMGs.

"He said that they were heavier sounding," Trujillo says, "louder, and more powerful."

So I switched out the pickups that were in my Tobias and I put EMGs in. That was it. From that point on, I was in for life. When I joined Ozzy's band, Zakk Wylde was using EMGs, so we always felt a kinship because we were both using EMGs. Then when I joined Metallica, obviously it continued.

For me, EMG always had the bite, the edge, and the power that really connects well to the style of music, the sound I needed, my style of playing, and the attack that I have on the strings. It was like the perfect marriage between the output of the pickup and the aggressive nature by which I played. The EMG pickup, to me, is like this little beast that lives in our instruments. It has its own personality, and for the kind of music we play, the style of playing that we create, it's compatible, but it's also its own personality. It's a versatile pickup, but it definitely has the edge and the attitude that we all like as players.

I've dabbled with other pickups, but I just felt that the output wasn't aggressive enough. That's just how it was. I came from aggressive bands, and I took that same sound and I applied it to the Infectious Grooves, which was more of an aggressive funk and metal sound. The pickup worked perfect for that. It translated well rather than being in a smooth kind of gentler vibe of soul and funk. I wanted it to be aggressive.

Some of my big influences have been players that had real aggressive tones, like Jaco Pastorius. But a lot of that sound came from using distortion and through his finger technique, which was playing really hard and close to the bridge. I could get all those things. But then I had the pickups that were an addition to those techniques. So I thought, "If I take this technique and apply it along with this pickup, it was like I was playing on steroids. It was my sound—but on steroids. And then, all of a sudden, it becomes a part of your DNA. You just get used to it. And it's a part of the journey that you take."

In 2020, after over thirty years of using EMG J sets, Trujillo and EMG made the partnership official and released the Robert Trujillo signature RT "Riptide" set. Rather than tweak what had long been Trujillo's signature sound, they attacked the pickup's look and added a custom regular or brushed chrome cap in silver or black.

"The concept for me was, again, the metal angle," continues Trujillo.

EMG has always had an incredible connection and rapport with Metallica and has always been open creatively to new ideas. Between me and Zach Harmon, my bass tech, we came up with some ideas that were very interesting to us. I actually have chrome basses, and we thought, "Why not add a chrome pickguard and then a chrome pickup?" It was a perfect visual match to the music. It was super slick and cool and also powerful. And again, [it] lent itself to the kind of music that we play.

The cool thing about Zach is that he gets very passionate about designs and aesthetics, and it has always got to be a great. I always trust his judgment. That's why Zach is the one who leads the connection to anybody that I'm dealing with—in this particular instance, Rob Turner. So Zach and I will get together, and we'll go over designs and ideas; then he'll take that to someone like Rob, and then they'll make it a reality. We get very passionate about our sound, so whatever we're attached to, it's important that everything about it is right. Zach is the guy who leads the charge. We trust him. Trust is huge. That's how we get done what we need to get done, and the final products are always over the top and amazing. It always exceeds our expectations, and that's through Zach."

Trujillo's long connection with EMG that predates his joining Metallica is a reflection of the mindset and values that made him the only person, after years of searching, who could fill the bass shoes left first by the tragic death of Cliff Burton and then by Jason Newsted's departure. Both Metallica and EMG were well established when Trujillo joined, but the band, the music, and their connection to EMG continue to grow. All the pieces feed off of and inspire each other.

"There's a continued growth," Trujillo continues.

We've all come up from where we've come up. And somehow, we've connected to the same place, whether it's our abilities as players or just creatively, in terms of the sound that we want and the product that we use. In all these relationships with these other like-minded individuals, a natural flow happens. It's that way with the musicians in this band and also with our techs and our engineers. It's how we record. We're all on the same mindset and wavelength, and our work ethic is the same. That's the great thing about Metallica, from every person that works on this crew to our engineering team—we always try to get the best of the best. We like to work with people that understand the work ethic, and EMG has everything to do with that same mindset. It's all about the quality of what we do and how we do it. Through that we can make great music, we can put on great shows, play at the highest level, and we can trust everything from our strings to our pickups to our amplifiers to our tennis shoes.

KIRK HAMMETT

What's left to say about Metallica and their relationship with EMG? The two more or less grew up together. On the wall of Alison Turner's office at EMG is a framed letter from the Metallica camp on photocopied Elektra Records letterhead, introducing the band and asking for their first endorsement. Kirk Hammett has gone from seeing EMG ads in magazines to being in those ads himself. What is there still to say about Metallica and their relationship with EMG? Apparently, there is a lot.

"I remember that initial drive up to Santa Rosa back in 1985," Kirk Hammett says, "meeting everyone at EMG and just checking these people out. They were a small operation, and I liked that because we were a small operation too. I could tell that they were a young company, they were hungry, and they really, really believed in what they were doing. That's how we were too. We were starting out, and 100,000 percent committed. We just wanted to make it happen, no matter what. When you hook up two entities that have that same sort of drive, good things come from it."

It's all about relationships. Metallica is a band that is—and always has been—built on relationships. The Metallica team from top to bottom is a family, and working through conflict, tragedy, and relishing the wins are what true families do.

The relationship between the player and the instrument, with the pickup being at the heart of that connection—the link, the transformer from vibrating air to electrical energy—lies at the heart of this book. And as long as

Metallica and Rob Turner continue to explore, push the edges, and are inspired by creation, their relationship will continue.

For Kirk Hammett, the magic came when the EMGs were paired with MESA/Boogie amps. That was the core sound. From there it's been about defining and refining that core sound. Headroom, gain, clarity, and sustain all combined to give both the intense clean sound and the sound on which to hang his heavy distortion and overdriven lead lines.

For years, Kirk used stock EMGs: 81/60s or the Super Strat–style S/S/81. At 2018's NAMM show, however, it was time for EMG to unveil a unique Kirk Hammett signature set: the KH BB, or Kirk Hammett Bone Breaker set.

"I was looking for something with just a little bit more bark," Hammett says.

> Something that was a little bit more reminiscent of the seventies-kind-of-Marshall sound but modernized. That's how the Bone Breaker set came about. For me, it's all about really, really tight low end and a really smooth high end. I like just a little pick sound when you hit the string. I don't like it too much, because, for me, it's a distraction.
>
> Another great thing about EMG pickups is that you can sit down with a frequency analyzer, pinpoint the frequencies, and EQ them out in real time, which is amazing to me. That's just so much more difficult to do with nonactive pickups because they don't have that constant "on-ness." With EMG you can get really subtle with it. You can dive in, in ways that are really cool. I also love the 81s because I think they're even more responsive to touch. If anything, I'm going to start another conversation with EMG about taking those even further.

Zach Harmon had his hand in creating Hammett's signature set too. "Some of Kirk's guitars had 81s, front and rear, some had 81/60s, some had at 81/85," says Zach. "Over time, I figured that we had to get Kirk some consistency so it wasn't like a certain guitar for a certain song. So we worked on something special for Kirk. We came up with the name and the artwork. Then Justin Crew, his guitar tech, put as many sets as we could into his guitars. Now Kirk's sound is solid. It's constant between all of the instruments."

At the time of this writing, in the middle of the COVID-19 pandemic, Metallica had created a bubble around their headquarters in San Rafael, California. The band and crew went through all the health and safety protocols and took advantage of the mandated world pause to connect and create. Imbedded within that process lies the search for new sounds.

Hammett shares the following:

When you go into the studio and start recording, all the gear comes out—all the gear—which means multiple guitars, multiple stacks of amps. Effects come out, rack gear comes out, obscure stuff comes out. I like to find effects that people have either forgotten about or don't use anymore so that they ask, "What is he doing? How is he getting that sound?" Usually, this is the time where we start thinking of how we can improve certain things or if there's anything that we want changed. And that's kind of got me to thinking about maybe revisiting the 81 and 60 and saying, "What can we do to maybe update it, maybe steer it in a certain direction?"

There's still work to do, still tone to explore, and Greeny (Kirk's very special 1959 Les Paul Standard) has a date with Rob in Santa Rosa. Some guitars are legendary. This guitar, originally owned by Peter Green of Fleetwood Mac and then by Gary Moore, has been called magic and not only because Green recorded the original version of "Black Magic Woman" with it. It's all about tone, and according to Hammett, "When you put the pickup selector in the middle, it sounds like a Strat. It's so crazy. Not a thin, jangly Strat, though, like a 'full-on / take-your-face-off Strat through a one hundred-watt Marshall at full volume' Strat." The plan is to put Greeny on Rob's bench and figure out just what exactly gives it that sound. (Read about Rob's investigation on Greeny in chapter 8.)

That guitar has had a lot of issues. It's had two of its pots changed. It's been refretted. The neck has been broken. And through all that, it still manages to retain its sound, and that is pretty amazing. I've had numerous people look it over. I've had Gibson do an MRI, and they all come to the same conclusion: "Not really sure why that guitar sounds the way it does." It's just one of those guitars, you know . . . yeah, it's just one of those guitars. There's a slight alteration to the pickup. But other than that, the sound has been documented since, like, 1965 or something like that, and it still sounds the same. What I want to do is to get into the nitty gritty of the tone and the tonal aspects, the frequencies, and sit down with Rob and have a real kind of, like, investigative conversation with him about that guitar's frequency and how and why it does what it does—because it's such a unique guitar.

"I feel very fortunate to have that guitar; that guitar found me. That guitar, it's just so much force, a real force of nature. And I just . . . I'm in awe of it. And it's because I'm in awe of it, I play it all the time. I can't keep my hands off it."

JAMES HETFIELD

And then there's the Het Set. If one story wraps up, defines, and can be used as the modern tone-chasing archetype, it's the evolution and creation of James Hetfield's signature EMG set: the Het Set. James had been a longtime 81/60 user. The 60 (part of the ill-fated pitch to Fender for their Elite series) in the neck position gave a clean yet powerful tone that, when paired with the high output of the 81 in the bridge position, provided Hetfield with the dynamic range to pull off Metallica's diverse and intense musical range—often in the same song. Check out "One" from *And Justice for All* for a sense of both the 81/60's and the band's combined muscle.

Evolution is one of the elemental attributes of a tone chaser. As James evolved as a player, got his hands on some iconic vintage guitars, and gained a deeper understanding of the electric guitar's intricacies, he began to wonder if there was more out there. Add to that a few catalysts that coalesced, which made the time right to see just where that 81/60, clean and dirty, rhythm/lead pickup combination could be pushed.

Hetfield shares the following:

> First, I knew Rob was basically a scientist and very, very up for a challenge. For me, I was at a point where I had very much gotten into that old-school humbucker, passive sound. I was able to collect some pretty important guitars, '59 Les Pauls, '58 Explorers, things like that. Obviously, you're not going to put EMGs into those. But I wanted to play them, and I wanted to incorporate that into my sound. The passive pickups made me play a little freer. But when I wanted to lock down and get into a fast down picking, they just didn't have what was needed.
>
> So I pitched that to Rob. I said, "I love the midrange freedom and the dynamics of these passive old pickups, but I missed that reliable crunch and smoothness that we've always had with an 81." So the challenge was put to him to come up with something.

With challenge accepted, Rob, James, and Zach Harmon set out to create magic. According to Harmon, the goal was to create a pickup set that combined the tight, crunchy EMG elements with the dynamics and responsiveness of those classic passive humbuckers that inspired Hetfield. With the 81/60 as the starting point, Hetfield and Harmon undertook a self-directed, advanced pickup education.

"I probably got one hundred sets of different pickups," Harmon says. "James would listen to them, and we'd get acquainted with different companies and different styles. James would translate to Rob what he was hearing and what he wanted. Rob was amazing. He just had this ability to know. You could tell his wheels were spinning and he was figuring out what he was going to design to get James what he was asking for. It took a long time, but I've got to tell you Rob made it."

A long time translates to three years. Being on the road for much of that time led to some challenges, but they established a rhythm where Rob would communicate with James, take the feedback, put together a prototype, send it to James and Zach for testing, and then repeat the cycle—seventeen times. Each pickup would be recorded via that band's Pro Tools rig. Zach would switch pickups in and out of the same guitars, same strings, and same recording setup so that everything was as consistent as possible, and the pickups could be compared on equal footing. James would play, listen, make notes, send them to Rob, and await the tweaks and adjustments to come.

"James got very, very specific," continues Zach. "He wants to hear the pick hit the string. He wants to hear every little imperfection or perfection in the note and his performance. He wants to hear the clarity of all that but not lose the bottom end. So Rob would listen, they would talk, and he'd come back with a new set. I'd pop them in, and James would know right away. He'd make up his mind in like two minutes about what he liked and didn't."

"It just had to be right," Hetfield says, "down to just tweaking little frequencies. Rob was very excited to have this challenge. I'm super stoked that it happened. And basically, I have not gone back. I haven't gone back to the other ones at all. This is my standard set."

Released in 2011, the JH Het Set is made up of two different pickups. The neck pickup took the standard EMG 60 and increased the attack and output and added a fuller low-end response. In the bridge pickup, Rob replaced the bar magnets in the 81 with steel polepieces, producing a cleaner low end with the tight attack common to the 81. Added to this were myriad adjustments and fine-tuning to the internal preamp and gain structure of both pickups.

The Het Set quickly became—and continues to be—one of EMG's best-selling pickup combinations. This continues the theme that first established itself when Hap Kuffner realized that he could sell the top-of-the-line guitar's engine and make that musical ethos available to any guitarist brave enough to take their instrument apart and tinker under the hood. For $250, the kids sitting in their bedrooms could take a budget Les Paul or Flying V copy and put in the same pickups that their idol used—not simplified, budget copies but the exact same pickups. While it takes a lot more than just pickups to sound like James Hetfield, it certainly gets one closer. Perhaps more important, it strengthens that connection between a player and their inspiration.

"I didn't have the awareness back when I was a kid," James says. "Pickups? I just wanted to know what kind of guitar it was. What did it look like? What color was it? The pickup was part of the sound, but it wasn't the key element. It's good to have that awareness that you can get 80 percent of the way there with this pickup. At least for me, I can put that set into almost any guitar and be 80 percent of the way to sounding like James Hetfield."

It's clear from talking with all involved that this whole process was a labor of love. Yet again, we've got professionals at the top of their games who still have the passion and love for their respective crafts that have sustained them for decades and continue to add fuel to their creative fires.

"It takes a real gift to listen and be creative," James continues.

A lot of creative people don't want to listen; they just want to do things their way. You know, sometimes I fall into that category as well. But Rob talks with the artists. He asks, "What are you missing from here? What would you like to hear that you don't?"

That's what Rob did with me, and I sought that out with him. I knew he was a scientist. I knew he was, like me, chasing that ultimate tone, ultimate sound, ultimate crunch. And I knew he was up for the challenge. So having someone that's able to listen and get what the artist is after and get the creative jolt of being a part of that, he's a very needed person. And it makes sense that he is where he is right now, so influential in the business. You know, musicians, they've got egos, and we don't like it when people say, "No." When I came to Rob and said, "Hey, I'd like to try this," he certainly didn't say, "No." He was up for a new challenge. That's what I love about him. He took that challenge, and he ran with it. And he ran way further than I had expected.

7

BROTHER BILL

Rob Turner: April 25, 1951, to November 11, 2011. My brother was one of those kinds of guys that did everything his own way. He didn't take a lot of advice. When he was a kid, he had a tricycle, but he wouldn't sit on it. He'd always put one foot on the back, both hands on the handlebars, and push himself down the street with the other foot. He just did his own thing.

He was an amazing mechanic, though; he would attack anything. He was the bicycle repairman, the custom model builder, the slot car builder. He was who he was. I don't know where he got all his ideas from. I have no idea.

He was a Taurus. I grew up with three Tauruses, and I was the last of four siblings, so I learned a lot about how to navigate my way through strong-willed people. I have a totally different personality than my brother. He was a perfectionist. He wanted everything done perfectly. I mean, there was no doubt that things had to be built right. He took his work very personally. When people would comment about what he did and the things that he created, he did not take criticism from people who were not directly attached to what he was doing. He would take criticism from Jeff Beck without question. But if some marketing guy said, "Well, we can't market this," or, "That doesn't really work," he would just look at him and go, "You know, you're an idiot." He would say it straight to their face. He wouldn't play the diplomatic, work-around game.

When it came to his guitars, he was a totally self-taught guitar player, and he could play amazingly well. He knew tone. He could play fingerstyle or with a pick. He taught himself how to play incredible guitar solos, and at the end of the day, he really didn't want to do too much else.

If Rob is this story's hero—the character who learns, grows, and undergoes change—then brother Bill plays the tragic hero's role—the character who wrestles his demons, and in the end, they prove too much to overcome. While this story is full of people who have searched for and found their tone, in many senses, brother Bill never truly did. That said, it's more than fair to say that there would be no EMG without Bill. Perhaps there would be, but it would certainly be a very different beast. Without his older brother and his Gibson ES-335, Rob may very well have found a different piece of electronic gear to take apart, mess with, and reassemble. Rob's connection to music would also likely not have been as strong. Without Bill and his friends needing a drummer and younger brother Rob being called into service, who knows whether Rob would have traveled down musical paths? What is certain is that Bill's and Rob's stories are intertwined. For years the name EMG was synonymous with Rob and Bill Turner. Although Bill's ending was tragic, the role he played, not only in EMG's early days but also in what he was able to add to the electric guitar's lexicon in his own right, deserves a closer look.

When Rob headed off to Portland for the ill-fated attempt to make it as a professional musician, Bill stayed behind in Sonoma County, met Patty Burnett, and the two married in 1974. Bill did odd jobs and Patty worked as an emergency room nurse. As Rob went through his trials and tribulations—the dead-end in Portland, heading back to live with mom and dad, looking for a product to sink his teeth into—Bill and Patty were making a life for themselves in Sonoma. They welcomed their first daughter, Nicole, into the world in December 1976 and their second, Julia, in 1978.

By 1976, as Rob was making Dirty Works pickups, Bill had made a connection with Redwood Audio Manufacturers, a high-end speaker and audio component company. He convinced one of their sales reps, Jim Boucher, to sell Dirty Works. Through Redwood's reputation and Boucher's natural sales abilities, they were able to get their pickups first into Stanroy Music Center in Santa Rosa and then into many other stores in the area. Rob had a rep covering Southern California, but the boys in the north were doing a much better job.

"We were advertising in *BAM*, Bay Area Music magazine," says Rob. "Jim was going to all the local music stores. He'd go to Stanroy, he'd go over to Oakland to Leo's Music Store and Don Wehr's in San Francisco—all of the stores in the general Bay Area. And we started selling product into these stores. I was making all this product in Long Beach. Eventually, it got to the point where most of the product we were selling was in the Bay Area, so Bill said, 'Well, this is going relatively well. Why don't you move up here?' I didn't want to be in LA anyway, so that's what I did."

Rob moved in with Bill, Patty, and Nicole, and the brothers ran EMG out of a bedroom in their house at 801 College Avenue in Santa Rosa. Soon second daughter Julia arrived on the scene. It was a tight fit, but it worked. Bill was in a good head space, the company was gaining traction, and times were exciting.

They moved from the place on College Avenue to a larger house on Village Side Street in the nearby neighborhood of Montgomery Village. EMG transitioned to a small outbuilding on the property. Moving the workshop out of the house gave space for the brothers to hire half-a-dozen employees to ramp up production. By 1982 they had moved again, this time to Villa Maria Court, in more of a suburban neighborhood. EMG, which by now was both the company and product name, moved out of the house and into a small, metal, garage-type unit in a nearby industrial area. This was the first time that the company and the house were separate entities—and also when tensions between the brothers started to mount.

At first Bill wasn't involved in the product design. Rob had brought all of the prototypes, drawings, and ideas with him when he moved up from Long Beach. Bill wasn't a draftsman either. Although their dad instilled in both brothers the importance of drawing, planning, and documenting ideas (especially necessary if one expects others to build a product), Bill didn't see the importance of this in the same way Rob did. As the company grew, however, his influence on the pickups' tone and design grew, and by 1982, his sonic fingerprints were as much on the company as Rob's.

Hap Kuffner joined the EMG team during those exciting early days while the brothers were a unified front, working together, and both the product and the company solidified. From Hap's point of view, the two brothers played very different but symbiotic roles.

"Bill was a true guitar geek," Hap says.

Rob was the guy with the soldering iron in his hand. Bill was very interested in getting ahold of every single guitar he could get his hands on, taking the pickups apart and seeing what made them work. Bill would take old, destroyed guitars, rip the pickups open, and see what kind of wire and magnets were there. He would do the research, talk to other guitar geeks, and then it would shift over to Rob to create the product. The two brothers worked in tandem. They were the first guys I knew who would set up an oscilloscope, measure the peaks and valleys of the pickup's output, and then dial that information into the preamp.

With the move to the new house, the separation of home and business, and Rob's blossoming relationship with Karen, cracks began showing in the brothers' relationship. There was a strange disconnect: sales were taking off, the company doubled its number of employees and then doubled again, but as success mounted, Bill became less and less interested in the company's inner workings.

Rob left his brother's house and moved in with Karen in 1982, and while his life would soon be anchored with a family of his own, Bill's personal life spiraled in the opposite direction. Cocaine, which had been a part of Bill's life since the early seventies, became even more present. The connection to the eighties rock-and-roll lifestyle made the drug easy to access—and plentiful. As his addiction grew, his personality changed, and all the relationships in his life suffered.

"It got to the point," says Rob, "where Bill would go over to the shop and spend all night by himself, just playing his guitar and doing coke. Patty and the kids would be at home, and she'd be understandably pissed off. Things just basically fell to pieces. It went from bad to worse, and he ended up leaving Patty and moved in with a friend, which only fueled his addiction."

Rob likes to say that Bill left the company physically in 1989 but that he had left in spirit in 1985. Between 1985 and 1989, Bill's contribution to the company dwindled to the point where he wasn't contributing to the pickup business anymore and was actually pursuing other products and designs.

"Bill was enamored with Ned Steinberger," Rob continues. "Steinberger played such a big role in our company, and Ned was a successful designer. Bill saw himself as a mechanical designer, too, and drew inspiration from

Ned. Around 1986 he started working on a replacement tremolo system for Stratocasters. It was a lot like the Steinberger TransTrem [Transposing Tremolo, which could be locked into place, essentially retuning the entire guitar up or down in pitch]." He couldn't get it quite right, but it started him toward other designs and away from EMG.

Bill's next idea built off the Steinberger straight-pull tuning system and gearless tuner Ned had developed. Rob told him, "Steinberger is one of our biggest customers. If you're going to do this, you can't do it here." And that was the end of Bill's relationship with EMG. Rob bought him out of the company, and Bill went on to start the Linear String Research (LSR) Company.

On March 24, 1992, Bill received patent no. 5097736 for his LSR tuners. The patent reads as follows:

> A tuning device includes a tuner housing extending from a string instrument, such as a guitar, with an integral orthogonal threaded mounting portion mounted in a peghead aperture. A tuner rod extends concentrically through the tuner housing and has a distal end with a transverse interior passageway extending at the end of the housing. A loose clamping pin or screw extends concentrically in the tuning rod to the transverse passageway. After a string end is pushed through the passageway and drawn taut a lock knob or the hex-headed screw at the tuner rod opposite end is threaded into the tuner rod forcing a separate or integral clamping pin against the taut end of the string and to clamp the string in the transverse passageway. An internally threaded tuning knob adjacent to the lock knob or hex-headed screw is rotatable on the outer threads of the tuner rod at its proximal end to move the tuner rod longitudinally inward in the tuner housing pulling with it the clamped string.

LSR tuners worked well. They had a much higher gear ratio, 40:1, compared to a standard tuner's 18:1, allowing for much more precise and stable tuning. They were lightweight and helped to alleviate neck dive in instruments with heavy headstocks or balance issues. Bill went further and designed the LSR Roller Nut, which also significantly increased tuning stability, especially when using tremolo bridge systems.

Bill took his knowledge of pickup design and tone and, in 1995, went to work for Fender's research and development department. He was instrumental in developing their Noiseless pickup line. These are essentially a humbucking pickup design but with the two coils stacked on top of each other to cancel the sixty-cycle hum rather than side by side in a conventional humbucking pickup. This allows them to retain the classic Fender single-coil pickup look while offering the clarity and punch of a passive humbucker. Eric Clapton is one the most famous proponents of Fender Noiseless pickups.

"To his credit," Hap Kuffner continues, "Bill did everything possible to make a high-impedance pickup noiseless and didn't put Fender into conflict with EMG. I've played modern guitars with Fender Noiseless pickups. Those designs were done by Bill Turner, and they're pretty darned good designs."

When asked about his product-development role at Fender in the March 3, 2003, edition of *Canadian Guitar Player*, Bill told writer Mark Grove: "The American Standard Strat, Tele, Jazz Bass, and P Bass all were upgraded with new pickup designs. MIM [Made in Mexico] guitars were upgraded with new pickups soon after, but the first major project undertaken was developing a new program for Fender Humbucking pickup designs." He adds that his history with EMG gives him "a unique perspective, having come from an audio and electronics engineering background" and that the key to Fender's success lies "in developing new materials for pickup design for the future."

Bill found a home at Fender. "He worked there for quite a while," Rob says, "and worked directly with Dan Smith and John Carruthers. He was pretty tight with John Page and the rest of the guys who were reinventing Fender at the time. It was a pretty tight little community." John Carruthers remembers that time fondly and speaks very highly of Bill's contributions, particularly his LSR Roller Nut.

Bending notes, creating vibrato, and all the various tremolo arms and whammy bars have long been problematic when it comes to keeping a guitar in tune. Unless the instrument is set up well and the string can move freely through the nut, when a sting's pitch is bent up or down (thereby changing its tension), often the string doesn't return to exactly the original pitch, throwing the instrument out of tune. With the eighties' and nineties' guitar gymnastics and bridge systems like the Floyd Rose Tremolo, this proved an even more significant challenge to overcome. Fender had worked with other companies to develop a nut system that allowed the string to move freely when bending notes, but there were issues.

"There were two different kinds of systems," says Carruthers.

The first one was just a single row of rollers. There were problems with getting different-sized string gauges to fit in them, so they were made specifically for a certain range of string sizes. The problem with rollers is that, in certain load circumstances, they work. But normally, when you've got a string that's barely making any kind of contact with it, it's just on the very apex of a curve, and the roller doesn't roll. The string just slides over the top of it. And because the slots were not snug enough on the string, you would get sizzling and weird noises that were unacceptable.

So they came up with a new version that had two rollers, and you'd zigzag the string through it. You'd go over the one roller and then under the other roller, and that put downward tension on it so it was pressing harder on the roller. That helped get rid of the unwanted noises, but bending the string to kind of a Z pattern brought extra problems as far as the string returning to pitch, and it would often go flat.

This was the challenge put before Bill, and he knocked it out of the park.

"Bill was very mechanically inclined," John continues. "And he had an idea." Bill asked John to source him an early version of a Floyd Rose tremolo system without the fine-tuning knobs that very early on became a standard feature of the design. Without the fine-tuning knobs on the Floyd Rose tremolo working in conjunction with the guitar's headstock tuners, getting and keeping the instrument in tune proved a real challenge. Bill wanted one, however, to test his theories about a nut system at the headstock that could allow the string to smoothly transition through both extreme and subtle pitch changes and return to its original pitch.

"I found an old one that didn't have the fine-tuners," John continues.

I gave it to him, and he started working on his design, and it was cool. It had two ball bearings that were in contact with each other. And the V that it created was the notch where the string would sit. Because of that design, you can put any gauge string you want within the width of the slide. There was a housing that had little hollow spots for the ball bearings to sit in. And then there was a clip that acted like a retainer that actually kept the ball bearings from falling out. And then, there was one other thing that made it all come together: it had a little sort of piece of neoprene that was right behind the ball bearings so that the string behind the nut would be damped and wouldn't cause unwanted sounds.

As a retrofit, you would need to cut away a little bit of the fingerboard to fit the nut's housing. Fender sold a kit with all the specifications and instructions required to make those adjustments. On Fender's own instruments, they could obviously make the adjustments in-house. The nut was standard on several Fender models and played by many—most notably, Jeff Beck. Today, Bill's LSR Roller Nut still receives rave reviews and is a standard feature of many acrobatic guitarists' setups.

Bill contributed to many other projects during his tenure with Fender. However, in 2006, he left the company and moved back to Santa Rosa. The Turner brothers cautiously reconnected. Bill would come by occasionally and jam, but it never went much further than that. Bill had remarried and had his addictions more or less under control, but there was too much water under an already-burned bridge for the two brothers to truly reconcile.

In 2010 Bill had a major stroke. He lost the ability to speak and most of the control of the left side of his body. He moved into a nursing home and, a little less than a year later, developed pneumonia, went into the hospital, and never made it out.

"He was only sixty, which is really sad," continues Rob. "It worked for a long time, and to tell you the truth, without the drugs, everything would have been different. It's amazing what drugs and alcohol can do to a person. So there you go. That's my brother. He did accomplish a tremendous amount, but basically, he was like a lot of people; he was just simply a victim of his choices, and that's not something that a lot of people have control over."

While brother Bill's story is a sad one, like all tragic heroes, there's a sense of loss for potential seemingly unfulfilled—he was there at the start and contributed in both significant and less obvious ways to not only EMG's story but also the world of music and musicians—an influence that can still be seen and heard to this day. He sacrificed a beautiful Gibson ES-335 to Rob's soldering iron. He accompanied Rob to see the Doors, the Grateful Dead, and Jefferson Airplane. He opened musical doors for Rob, which otherwise would likely have stayed shut. Perhaps most important, he was instrumental in establishing EMG in the Bay Area, which led to the many connections with Bay Area musicians who put those little, black, active pickups on the map. He took his brother in and, along with his wife Patty, provided the early foundations for the company to flourish. RIP, brother Bill.

8

SOMETIMES YOU JUST LEAVE IT ALONE— BUT MORE OFTEN YOU EXPLORE

Bernhard Kurzke: Of course, we always have to hold him back. Rob is super friendly. I've seen it many times. He'll be at a show talking to a major distributor from some country or another, and somebody will come over and say, "Oh, I have a problem. This didn't work properly, or that didn't work." Rob will say, "Sorry, just hang on a minute," to the big distributor and answer the player's question. If a musician asks him something crazy like, "Do you do a left-handed, seven-string version of that pickup in pink? Is that possible?" Rob will say, "Oh, yeah, there's nothing that is impossible."

Since the beginning the challenge has fueled the adventure. Combine a challenge with the opportunity to work with passionate, equally driven creators, and you've hooked Rob pretty much every time. In many ways EMG mirrors a record label or a traditional publisher's business structure. They have their group of core products, which is often surprisingly small. That small group of core products provides the financial stability to take on smaller passion projects, gives space for experiments to fail, and allows Rob to take on tasks that fuel his creativity. The beautiful element at play is the symbiotic relationship between art and commerce. Projects feed off and support each other, often in unexpected ways. The unpredicted twist that uncovers the right voice for a player's guitar pickup might end up being the missing tonal recipe for a unique bass instrument's design as well.

The obscure challenges have always had the strongest hold on Rob. His love is being able to be creative. Tom Ribbecke, luthier of Bobby Vega's, Joel Landsberg's, and Jack Casady's Halfling basses, tells of how Rob jumped on board the pickup project for Tyler Wells's multiscale Nate Lopez guitar. Tyler honed his luthier trade working as Ribbecke's apprentice. According to Tom, Tyler is the best he'd ever had. Not only are his skills prodigious, but he's also taken the master's work, added his own spark, and taken the instrument designs further.

"Tyler asked me how to approach Rob," Ribbecke says.

> Tyler was only in the business for a little while, and his only credit was that he was working for me. This is what touches me most about Rob. He rolled out the red carpet for Tyler. There was really no commercial interest. He wasn't going to make money. It was about Rob wanting to know what Tyler was doing, handling him completely, and wanting to put beauty on the planet. No matter how you look at it, that's why we do this. We're going to leave a body of work that's going to outlive us, and maybe it will be "Beauty: 1, Ugly: 0" for the tools I left here. That's why I do what I do, and I know Rob has the same mindset, although I think he is a lot more organized than me.

"Here's a great story," says Rob. "Do you have your tape recorder running?"

Back in the day, those inclined to take on home guitar repair or modifications needed a soldering iron always at the ready. For some this isn't a barrier. For many the thought of heating up a metal wand to over 600 degrees Fahrenheit, melting a mixture of tin and lead, and joining together wires or other electronic components is more than enough to send one running to their nearest guitar repair shop. After the active pickup itself, solderless wiring connections may be EMG's most significant contribution to the art of personalizing the electric guitarist's arsenal.

Since 2009 EMG pickups, switches, preamps, and wiring have employed a series of connector clips that can be joined together as simply as plugging an electrical cord into a wall socket. A few years earlier, the path towards a truly complete, self-contained, plug-and-play system started like many innovations do—as a response to a need, with a little serendipity mixed in. Rob explains,

We were producing a lot of pickups, and we would keep them on cookie trays. We would pot the pickup with [encase it in] epoxy so that everything would stay solid. But there was a cable coming from the pickup that the epoxy would wick up. There would be this one-inch, really stiff piece of cable because the epoxy had wicked up it. So we had to seal off the cable after we built the pickup.

On top of that, we were using alligator clips to hook them up and test them. You'd have to hook up one, and then you'd have to unhook it and get the next one. It was tedious and tiring. There would be these trays with thirty-some-odd pickups on each tray. The cables were all hanging everywhere. They would get caught on stuff. It was actually dangerous and a real mess.

At the time, Evans, a Canadian pickup company led by Rod Evans, was making a pickup with a three-pin connector. Rob loved the idea and replaced the wire coming out of the epoxy with a similar connector system. This type of connector wasn't new. Connectors of this sort had been used for years in all kinds of electrical systems. After some research Rob decided on a three-pin connector from Berg, a St. Louis company specializing in connectors for computer hardware.

"It was very tight. It went on, and it stayed on," he says. "So I designed the circuit boards in the pickups to have a Berg connector on the bottom. Then when we tested them, all we had to do was plug on the connector's other end. No more repetitive stress with alligator clips. The pickups sat on the trays without cables. No more mess. It just became so much easier to have a connector on the bottom of the pickup."

All was going well. Then an email arrived out of the blue, and things got even better.

"I've searched for the email," says Rob.

I can't remember exactly when it came or who it was who sent it, but it basically said, "Hey, what are you doing? You put a connector on the bottom of the pickup. Why don't you put connectors on everything else? Put connectors on the pots, put connectors on the jack . . . Why don't you?" The email ended with something like, "I don't know how to solder, and I don't want to solder."

I just took this email to heart. They were absolutely right—we should! We had the first part of it. Why shouldn't we take it to the next level? It took a year or so to figure it all out, and then the big questions came: How do we sell this? How do we tell people that this is really a great thing? How do we convince people that they can change their pickup easily?

We landed on the idea that pickups could be like trading cards. Typically, every guitar player has a box full of stuff. If they've got a pickup and it's got a connector, and they've got a buddy who doesn't like their pickup, they could swap.

In the end it went much further than that. Just ask Zach Harmon how much easier the connector system made the Het Set creation process. Beyond simplifying life for the guitar techs, the solderless connector system made the world of sound, tone, and instrument personalization accessible to just about any player.

Throughout EMG's evolution there has always been a push and pull, an almost cat-and-mouse relationship between technology, the changing music business, and Rob's work. In one moment an advancement in technology drives a change in instrument design, which, in turn, impacts the music store shelves. Just as often, a superstar musician, band, or genre will open up a new space in the marketplace, leaving builders to create products that appeal to the masses. There are even times when the builder creates a product that the hot players grab onto, and the market falls all over itself to make that product available to all.

As the music business changed from mom-and-pop stores to nationwide conglomerates (the marketplace driving innovation), EMG, as one of the foundational pickup companies, survived, even thrived, as Rob explains, "because we were on vinyl." Solderless connectors provided an unexpected and unintentional bonus and a ready-made harmonious connection to changes in the music business that were only beginning to be realized when EMG shifted their production in 2009.

From kids circling the Silvertone guitar in the Sears catalog to manufacturers sharing their latest products with distant markets, catalogs had long played a role in matching players with gear. Their significance became even more impactful as the music business shifted and conglomerated through the nineties and into a new century. Musician's Friend, American Music Supply, Sam Ash, and others gave access via mail-order to a music store unencumbered by bricks and mortar and stocked with almost anything a player could need.

Add the internet into the equation, and very quickly, the entire game has changed. Now the largest music dealers on the planet, like Sweetwater Sound,

Zzounds, Guitar Center, Musician's Friend, Cosmo Music, and even Amazon, take up very little physical real estate. Even the used-gear marketplace has been digitized, with Reverb and eBay leading the way. It's hard to imagine anything that can't be found online.

For years many automatically believed that instruments, particularly high-end instruments, could only be bought in person. They needed to be picked up, held, played—loved at first strum. While it's safe to say that is no longer always the case, accessories like strings, electronics, straps, picks, and so forth never had problems finding customers from afar.

Rob's vision for solderless electronics unintentionally moved the EMG catalog even more firmly into that easily accessible accessory marketplace. In almost the same amount of time it took to change a set of strings, you could now swap out a pickup and open up a new world of tone. As the entire musical instrument marketplace became an open twenty-four-hours, seven-days-a-week, from-the-comfort-of-your-living-room experience, EMG was already there with a product that didn't require a trip to the local guitar tech to install. On top of all that, the group Rob envisioned swapping pickups like trading cards is alive and well and connected worldwide through social media.

Uncovering the pickup recipe that will fill and fire the soul is very much like searching for buried treasure. Sometimes, there's a well-worn path to the hiding place with a fully detailed topographical survey. Other times, there are only the faintest of rumors that the bounty even exists, and the map is faded with terrifying renditions of sea monsters guarding the X that marks the spot. Regardless of parameters and even though it's often up to those on the search to draw it, there's always a map. When you've been lucky enough to grab Rob's attention and he's committed to the chase, his first request will be to play your instrument.

"Bring your instrument in," he says. "I need to listen to it, and the only way to really listen to it is to put it up against your ear, push it up against your eardrum, and hit the thing." That's been the first step since the beginning. The feedback often leads in unexpected directions, like when the unamplified sound of the original Steinberger L2 carbon-fiber composite bass led Rob to add midrange to the pickup, the opposite of what the vast majority of basses require.

"That's pretty much the way that it starts. Every instrument has a timbre, and you can tell right away whether the particular instrument will ever give you the sound that the player wants. Some instruments are virtually impossible to get what the player is looking for. If that's the case, I wouldn't even say that you could put a different bridge on or do something else. No matter what you do—change the bridge, change the nut, change, change, whatever—it's not going to get there."

After recognizing and naming the instrument's natural, unamplified acoustic sound; realizing that it has a specific quality; and committing to the exploration, a series of questions follow.

What's the first thing that you plug into? That's the first question I ask. What's at the front end that you plug your instrument into? Do you plug into a tuner? Are you going directly into an amp? If you're starting with an effect or anything that has electronics in it, does the effect have an active bypass or a passive bypass? Many effects want to maintain the output impedance of the effect, so if you plug a high-impedance pickup into it, it actually has a low-impedance output when you bypass it.

Next, what kind of amp and what kind of speakers are you using? It's also really important to ask, What's your environment? Where are you playing? Are you playing in your bedroom? Do you play with a bunch of friends in a big room? What kind of rig do you have for recording, and what kind of a rig do you have for live performance? For example, when you're dealing with a bass, if you're in a studio, you typically don't need anywhere near the low end that a bass needs live. You just need a solid tone coming out of the instrument. If you look at some of the Beatles' recordings, Paul McCartney is playing through a Fender Bassman amp, and he's got a condenser mic in front of it. It's only six or eight inches away from the speaker cabinet. There's no low end right there. You don't get any low end until you're at least four feet from the cabinet, and then you start to hear the low end. Recording is such a different process than playing live.

Then, how do you play? Do you play with a pick? Hetfield uses a really unique pick and picking style. A lot of bass players play with a pick. Some don't. Jack Casady hits with the ends of the fingers. He has this sort of slap thing that he uses. Phil Lesh plays with a pick. Bobby Vega plays with a pick and his fingers.

That's the start of the process. It starts with the instrument. Then it moves on to a review of the environment. Once those two aspects are nailed down, Rob moves on to the actual sound, the tone the player seeks. That's when the fun actually begins.

He asks, "Okay, well, how big and beefy do you want this to be? What kind of music are you playing? Where do you fall in the mix with the people you play live with? Where do you want to be in the mix when you record?"

The more beautiful the questions, the more beautiful—or impactful or face-ripping—the sonic answers will be. Rob continues,

> The first thing I do is determine the size of the pickup's aperture, the amount of physical space available. Then I can pretty much build something up from there. For instance, if a bass player says, "I need a lot of midrange because I'm mostly a ballad player. I want a little boost in the low end and not a lot of high end, but I want some punch out of it too," that's tricky because it's actually two or three different things. If you want punch out of it, you need to have the magnet directly under the strings. If you use a setup like a P Bass or a Jazz Bass, punch is not really something that enters into the equation unless you have a lot of space for the pickup.

The aperture and pickup housing size are important. A smaller housing, like a typical single-coil Strat or J Bass, can limit the available options. You can get away with a lot more with a larger, humbucker-sized opening. A larger pickup housing can even cover a smaller pickup. For example, the Steinberger bass pickups are basically a traditional P Bass-style pickup in a humbucker housing.

"You can think of the process as creating a mixture. We might want to make gray. We start there, but then do you want it to be on the light side, on the dark side, or somewhere in between? When we start talking in colors, I find that the artist and I start to understand each other."

Once Rob starts talking colors, the wheels start turning. Punch comes from the amount of steel in the magnet. The actual magnetic strength plays a pivotal role. Measured in gauss (abbreviated as G or Gs, named after German mathematician and physicist Carl Friedrich Gauss), the pickup's magnetic strength directly correlates to the perceived brightness. In simplest terms, the stronger the magnet, the brighter the pickup sounds. Pickups' gauss readings vary greatly. Typically, Fender guitar pickups are the strongest, with the Jazzmaster measuring over 1,000 gauss. Stratocasters and Telecasters vary from just under 1,000 to around 650, depending on the alnico blend. Classic Gibson pickups are significantly weaker, with a P-90 measuring just over 250 gauss and a PAF (Patent Applied For) usually around 225. A standard Gibson humbucker reads 300 to 400 gauss.

How many pickups are on the instrument? How close are they to the neck and the bridge? What kind of strings does the player use? With the starting point nailed down and an agreed-upon common language in place, Rob then puts something together for the artist to try.

"There's a lot to consider," Rob continues. "But at some point, you just have to say, 'Okay, here, take the instrument, play it, and then come back and tell me what works, what doesn't work, and then we'll move on.' The fix could be as simple as just moving the coils closer together. It might be that I make a coil that's taller and skinnier instead of sort of fat and squat. I can jump to a different thing altogether and choose a different magnet material. I'll either have an aha moment and know what I need to do or have a suspicion and say, 'Okay, well, let's go in this direction and let's see what happens.'"

With luck, it comes together relatively quickly. Sometimes, however, Rob gets thrown a curveball. Grateful Dead guitarist Bob Weir offered up a particular challenge. More specifically, Weir's choice of strings muddied the waters.

"He uses Pyramid strings that are really odd," Rob says.

The low *E* is big and fat, almost like a bass string, but they're really flimsy strings. They're really floppy. I don't know how to really describe it, but they're like wet noodles. Also, the four wrapped strings are flatwounds, not roundwounds.

When Bob came and asked me to design a pickup for him, I had to have those strings on his guitar with him playing it. You couldn't just put a standard .046 to .010 gauge set on a guitar and say, "Let's see how this works."

Sometimes that aha moment takes him in completely unnatural directions that end up hitting the mark—Bobby Vega's Ribbecke bass, for example.

"For starters, it's acoustic," says Rob.

They didn't want to put too big of a pickup on it. There were all kinds of limitations in the size and mounting. It was like they wanted me to paint a Mona Lisa but gave me a canvas the size of a postage stamp. I started by using a really squat design with two coils right next to one another. The pickup was maybe an inch thick and was almost all coil. The preamp was actually about half the size of your little finger and about as thick as a matchstick. We started with alnico. And Bobby was like, "This thing just doesn't work."

The thing about those instruments—about the bass instruments in general—is that the pickup doesn't need to be compensated. There are no plain strings on the instrument, and they're all wound. So they all have the same timbre. They're all very linear. It's not like trying to do an acoustic guitar, where you have a high *B* and a high *E* that need to be compensated for because they're plain strings and not damped by wrapping around the string.

So we tried alnico, and it just did not have the dynamics that we thought it was going to have. There was plenty of magnetism, maybe 400 gauss, but the pickup was pretty far away from the strings. So he basically just said, "Well, this isn't working," and I said, "Well, I'll tell you what. I know this is odd, and this is not something I would normally do, because this is a bass, but let's put a couple of ceramic magnets in place of the alnicos, just to give it a try." Luckily, it worked.

At the end of the day, perhaps the biggest, most revealing, and valuable question is "Why?" Why is your tone not there yet? Is it simply because you're not happy with what you have? Or are you looking for a new muse, something that's different to launch off in a different direction?

"It's a unique, a very individualized unique process," Rob explains.

I don't always win. I've done stuff for people that they put on their instruments, and they love it. I'll do the same thing to another instrument of theirs, and it's a no-go. It just doesn't work in every situation.

We did a bunch of work on Oteil Burbridge's basses for a Dead & Company tour. He's a big EMG user. The first picture on his website's equipment page has a Modulus Graphite bass with EMGs. But for that tour, EMGs just didn't fit in the mix, and he swapped them out almost right away.

There have been surprisingly few failures over the years. Rob considers situations like Oteil's a failure mostly because the players don't come back. Bob Weir was tricky to work with too. He'd leave the shop, all would seem fine, but then he'd come back a few weeks later, and things wouldn't be quite right. They never could pin down and articulate exactly what wasn't working. In Rob's estimation, the following is true:

Simply not being able to satisfy an artist, that's kind of a grand failure. I mean, my first banjo pickup was a total failure. Probably my second one was too. I've had a couple of things that I've started that I've abandoned, but usually I don't give up until I've proven to myself that it's not going to work.

The other thing is that it might work from a sound point of view, but it might not work from a business point of view. If it's a custom job for a specific player and it's a challenge, okay, fine, no problem. I'll do what I can. We'll see how it works, and then we'll make it happen. But when we look at a project from a business point of view, I have to really be sure that I want to follow through and take the production all the way to the finish line.

And then there are some instruments that you simply just don't mess with. While many years ago there may have been no hesitation to cut up what today would be considered a vintage Gibson ES-335 TDN, over the years a handful of instruments have become ones that Rob simply says, "Leave them alone—they are what they are and are best left that way." Take, for example, Rickenbacker basses.

"Rickenbackers are unique," says Rob.

The timbre of the strings is all different. Put the bass to your ear and play it. You'll hear that the low E has a certain tone. Then hit the A string, and it just sounds like it's off a different instrument altogether. Then the D and the G, and as you fret up into the different positions, you still have different timbres. It's actually a good thing to have a pickup on there that has a small amount of magnetism (a typical Rickenbacker bass pickup measures approximately 200 gauss) and a coil that's pretty indistinct because then those different timbres all get balanced out. If you put a high-fidelity pickup on that bass, you're going to hear the differences in the strings. I've done it before, and that's why we don't do it anymore.

It comes down to the uniqueness of the instrument. If the guitar or bass is a one-of-a-kind instrument or has an identifiable tone all its own, perhaps it's best to leave it alone. Keep the irreplaceable tone machine in the arsenal, pull it out when it's needed, and experiment with other instruments. The instrument's age is not too much of a factor, although, admittedly, Rob's "ruined a lot of expensive guitars," especially in the early days. Vintage instruments that are simply old don't hold the same reverence as a classic guitar with a legacy and sound to match.

Some guitars gain notoriety for their sound. Clapton's Blackie, cobbled together from three different Stratocasters; George Harrison's 1963 twelve-string Rickenbacker; and Billy F. Gibbons' 1959 Les Paul, better known as Mistress Pearly Gates, all fit that bill. Others become famous for the way they look, just as much as for their tone. Van Halen's red, white, and black Frankenstrat, Bo Diddley's cigar-box guitars, and even Kurt Cobain's Jag-Stang defined their era's sounds and went a long way to set the visual standard for stadium rock, blues, and grunge, respectively. Hundreds of others fall into either of those categories, and a few cross the line between both. The 1959 Les Paul Standard, better known today as Greeny, falls into that category of the iconic instrument both instantly recognizable and sonically unmistakable.

Greeny started out in the hands of Peter Green, who reportedly purchased it secondhand in 1966 for around $300. Green had recently replaced Eric Clapton in John Mayall and the Bluesbreakers, catapulting the young British guitarist to instant fame. While relatively common and easy to find in the mid-sixties, this particular Les Paul was different. Individually, the pickups have the customary thick, warm Les Paul sound—fuller and rounder in the neck position, brighter with more bite in the bridge. Since the standard Les Paul pickups are wired in parallel, when the pickup selector switch is set to the middle on most Les Pauls, the tone gets a little more nasally, and the player can use the volume controls to blend which pickup (neck, or bridge, full or biting) adds the most character.

Greeny is different. When the middle pickup selector is chosen, the two pickups are out of phase. Rather than blending the tone, the pickups cancel specific frequencies, giving that sound Kirk Hammett calls "a full-on-take-your-face-off Strat through a one hundred-watt Marshall at full volume sound."

Green's tenure as a Bluesbreaker only lasted until 1967. He left the group and formed the original Fleetwood Mac alongside slide guitarist Jeremy Spencer, bassist Bob Brunning (replaced almost immediately by John McVie), and drummer Mick Fleetwood. It was with Fleetwood Mac that the 1959 Les Paul, with the very un-Les Paul-like sound's legend, began on tunes such as "Albatross," "Dragonfly," "Oh Well," and "The Green Manalishi (With the Two Pronged Crown)."

Tragically, Green suffered from well-documented bouts of mental illness. By the early seventies, he had lost interest in music. Wanting his beloved Les Paul to end up in good hands, he sold it to then up-and-coming Irish blues virtuoso Gary Moore. Moore took the guitar into his new band, Thin

Lizzy; featured it throughout his solo career; and eventually sold it in 2006 for reportedly between $750,000 and $1.2 million.

As classic song after classic song came out of the guitar, the myths as to why it sounds the way it sounds grew. Green claimed that he was responsible for reinstalling the pickup the wrong way around. Others said that at some point, a repair was done, and the pickup was rewound incorrectly. Ultimately, it's been agreed upon that the pickup's miswiring, resulting in the out-of-phase response, was done in error at the factory. Jol Dantzig, the noted guitar tech who co-founded Hamer Guitars, claims to have confirmed this when he did a diagnostic inspection of the guitar in 1984. According to Dantzig, although it's uncommon, other Les Pauls from that era have the same mistake.

Greeny's legacy doesn't end there, of course. In 2014 one of the heroes of this story, Kirk Hammett, ended up with the guitar, paying, according to some sources, in the neighborhood of $2 million. And while the mystery of when the unintentional error that led to the iconic tone occurred may have been solved, the mystery of just exactly how and why it sounds the way it does remained, which is why it ended up on Rob's workbench.

The connection between Kirk, Rob, and this iconic guitar coming together in the spirit of discovery, as well as those initial explorations with brother Bill's ES-335, are obvious—a melding of curiosity and inquisitiveness (this time, Rob's and Kirk's) facilitated by a mutual friend—in this case, Zach Harmon.

The first test involved hooking the guitar up to a frequency spectrum analyzer. Rob ran a signal through a pair of small coils that sat over the top of Greeny's pickups to measure their resonance. Next, a gauss test determined the amount of magnetism. Finally, Greeny was connected to a custom machine Rob built. In most cases he'd remove the pickup, but he left Greeny's in the guitar and struck the pickup with a piano key-and-hammer mechanism. This not only told Rob a lot about the pickup but also a tremendous amount about the resonance of the entire guitar as a system. Both these tests and a comprehensive forensic examination revealed many of Greeny's secrets.

"For starters," Rob says, "the guitar doesn't have a lot of resonance to it. It's actually relatively dead. It's a rocker guitar for sure, but there isn't a ton of natural sustain. The front pickup isn't actually wired backwards. It's just turned backwards. It's still the original pickup and hasn't been changed. The rear pickup has been opened. It has a different cable coming out of it, and the magnetism is reversed, which causes it to go out of phase in the middle position. Everything is very typical for a '59 Les Paul. The magnetism measures 250 gauss at the top of the polepieces. That's pretty low, which gives it a nice, smooth touch."

With the guitar safely back in Hammett's possession and the forensic diagnoses complete, Rob has no plans to recreate the pickups. As James Hetfield said, with the Het Set he's 80 percent of the way to his sound. To recreate Greeny's pickups, even to their exact specifications; wire them faithfully to the original misstep; and put them in any guitar other than that same Les Paul that had traveled down some incredible rock-and-roll roads, you still wouldn't get all the way to the tonal destination. You might get close, but 80 percent isn't close enough to call the journey complete, and there are other roads to explore. (Note: In March 2023, Gibson actually did release a Greeny replica, true to the original specs with recreated pickups and a $19,999 price tag. Rob wasn't involved in the process.)

CHASING TONE—
THE ARTISTS' JOURNEY
PART 4

Bobby Vega & Victor Wooten

Chasing tone in its purest and most rewarding form is an all-in endeavor. It engages the entire player: head, heart, and hands. The hands provide the physical connection to the instrument and sound generation. The head analyzes, compares, and contrasts. The heart knows what's true. Without getting too metaphysical, I can say both from personal experience and speaking with countless other musicians over the years, it's magic when the head, hands, and heart align and express that connection as music. Perhaps this has to do with vibrations. Since music is all about combining vibrations, playing with tension and release, perhaps that magic is merely a measure of the harmony or disharmony of those vibrations.

While all the artists who've shared their stories in these "Chasing Tone" sections reflect that harmonious marriage of musical vibrations, these final two are permanent residents of this world. They've carved paths by being uncompromising in the edict that music's goal is to be of service to itself and to be a vehicle of joy. Both have a sound and style that is instantly recognizable, but as players, they would never inflict a sound or a technique into a situation where the music didn't absolutely demand it. As the final two "Chasing Tone" artists, I can't think of two players better than Bobby Vega and Victor Wooten that sum up the elusive, personal quest for one's sound.

BOBBY VEGA

Once some tone chasers find their sound, the game is over. They're done. That's their sound, and they're sticking to it. For others, the game isn't to chase tone; it's to let tone find them. For that latter group, the strategy is to be open and aware, to listen for what the music calls for, and to be able to recognize what they need to do to complete that musical expression. Bobby Vega belongs to that latter group. From vintage Fender Jazz Basses to the ultra-modern Ribbecke Halfling acoustic bass, from pick to fingerstyle to thumb slapping, Vega employs whatever sound the music demands.

Music found Bobby early. Growing up in San Francisco during the sixties and seventies infused Vega with a cornucopia of sounds and styles. And he soaked it all in. At fifteen, he played with Bo Diddley. He achieved serious attention in musical circles a year later when he debuted his signature funk-heavy, picked-and-muted bass line that stole the spotlight on Sly and the Family Stone's "I Get High on You," the first track on their 1975 album *High on You*. He's gone on to play with an equally rich cornucopia of musicians, including Billy Preston, Booker T., Paul Butterfield, Joan Baez, Jerry Garcia, Bob Weir, Mickey Hart, Santana, Tower of Power, and Etta James, to name just a few.

His first bass was a Gibson EB-1. "I saw the band Mountain, and Felix Pappalardi was playing an EB-1," Vega says. "When I bought my first real bass, I had the choice between a Fender Telecaster bass and an EB-1. I picked the EB-1. That EB-1 got me fired from more gigs because you couldn't hear a note I played. It was so low-endy. Then I got a Jazz Bass, and everything opened up."

Bobby isn't exaggerating when he says that everything opened up when he found the Fender Jazz Bass. He's owned many over the years. Perhaps his most famous is his 1961 Jazz with the coveted concentric pots. He found it at Norman's Rare Guitars (then located in Reseda, California) in 1973 and traded a 1957 Jazz Bass with an anodized pickguard plus one hundred dollars for it. It's far from stock. The original bridge was replaced with an early version of the Leo Quan Badass Bass II bridge. The original pickups were replaced with a handmade set following a secret recipe he still won't disclose. If all of that didn't make it unique enough, in an effort to slow the finish wear on the back, Vega put a shark sticker on the back of the body. To this day, the Shark Bass holds a place of prestige among other iconic basses.

He was first introduced to EMGs in the late seventies during EMG's Overlend period.

"I bought a 1966 Jazz Bass at Leo's Music Store in Oakland, California. I didn't really like the way the original pickups sounded. They said, 'We've got some EMGs,' and put them in the bass. I knew I was looking for something different in my bass without routing it. I didn't know what I didn't like about the original pickups, but the first thing that somebody said to me when I played the EMGs was how even it was. I still have that bass. The pickups have changed now to the X series because I helped build them."

Bobby is also not exaggerating when he says that he helped build the bass versions of the EMG X series. He lives in Healdsburg, only about ten miles north of EMG headquarters. The way Bobby tells the story, back in 2008, Rob called him out of the blue for some advice on a project. They got to talking about life and the bigger picture. Bobby was tired of being on the road, one thing led to another, and Rob brought Vega into the company to help with development and exploration.

Vega became EMG's resident bass expert and provided Rob with invaluable insight from the player's mindset. He gave Rob access to a plethora of basses, both vintage and modern. More important, Vega could manipulate the instruments, pulling different tones out by picking, slapping, tapping, or using his fingers—any bass technique was easily accessible.

"Rob could make any kind of pickup sound," Bobby continues. "I've got a '58 P Bass. I've got a '55 P, a '60 P, a '65, and on and on. And they're all great examples of those instruments, and I know how to manipulate them. Whenever he wanted, Rob could hear the history of all those instruments because they were right there in the office."

Rob incorporated that knowledge into the products. The Geezer Butler signature model, for example, is based on Vega's 1960 Fender Precision Bass. The most significant element Rob pulled from Vega—and the one Bobby is most appreciative of—is that Rob simply let Bobby Vega be Bobby Vega. He got to play, explore, discover, refine, fail, and contribute to rich discussions and dialogues about his greatest passion: making the bass guitar sound wonderful.

"Rob related to me as a musician," Bobby says.

He was great to work for because he let me be me. He got to hear instruments. When Ned Steinberger came, I would help Ned. When Harvey Citron would come, I'd help Harvey Citron. I was a walking and talking book that had a history of instruments, knew where the balances were, and knew the different needs of different players.

I was fortunate and lucky to work with Rob for almost eight years. He understood me and gave me support. I'd do the research for him. I was a good machine for that because once you put something in my hand, he got to hear what it did. And then instead of me judging anything, he could take it from there.

I took EMGs over to Europe, all over the world, and all over the States. I played the NAMM show one year, and I had a set of EMGs in a Fodera bass. They wanted me to have a Bobby Vega signature model. I had EMGs in an MTD [Michael Tobias Design] 535 and a 445. I had EMG[s] in an F Bass. So in one NAMM show, I had everything from a '72 Jazz Bass with EMGs to a Fodera custom bass with EMGs. That's why a lot of people equate me with EMGs, but I never endorsed them. I just worked with Rob to raise the awareness of the pickups.

While it may seem surprising for Vega to say that he never endorsed EMGs, the point he's getting at is not only what makes him such a unique, inventive, and sought-after player, but it is also what made his contributions to EMG so invaluable. Vega is the antithesis of the player who finds his sound and never changes. It's not about endorsing a product; it's about recognizing when the right product arrives. He's always open, available, and ready to serve whatever musical situation he's in. That's why he's amassed a collection of instruments that would impress even the most jaded collector. His thoughts on the relationship between instrument and player can serve as sage advice for any musician.

"The sound is in my hands," he says.

And I go to the instrument. The instrument doesn't go to me, because the instrument can't go to you. That's not a secret. But it's so far away in most people's brains. You know, there's no such thing as a bad instrument. It just doesn't do what you want it to do. Then the question is, "How can you get it to do what you want?"

For me, it's a different kind of identification. It's all individual. The same instrument in somebody else's hand won't sound the same. Once I find something that sounds good, that's it. I've got another instrument to use. That's how I've ended up with so many basses. They all do something different. If they all had EMGs, it would be like always eating cheese sandwiches. They'd all sound the same.

The thing is that you don't pick the instrument; it picks you. You adjust to it, and then you become one with it. And how do you know when you've got it? When people react. It's not up to you. That's my observation over decades. You have to be able to change, to support the story you're telling. So that's that. There are differences, and everybody goes about it a different way, but that's the beauty of it."

VICTOR WOOTEN

There was never really any doubt that Victor Wooten would live a musical life—he was literally born into it. The youngest of five brothers, he started playing music at two; by five, he was gigging with his family band; and by six, the Wooten Brothers band with Victor on bass was on tour, opening for soul music legend Curtis Mayfield. In his official biography, Victor states, "My brothers, who were already playing music, knew they needed a bass player to complete the family band. Regi started teaching me as soon as I could sit up straight, and my parents let him do it."

Before Victor had finished high school, the Wooten Brothers band—with brothers Regi on guitar, Roy on drums, Rudy on sax, Joseph on keys, and Victor on bass—had shared the stage with Stephanie Mills, War, Ramsey Lewis, Frankie Beverly and Maze, Dexter Wansel, and the Temptations, to list just a few.

As a solo artist, a member of Béla Fleck and the Flecktones, and as a contributor to an almost endless list of A-level performers, Victor has carved out a place as one of the most-respected, influential, and celebrated contemporary bassists. He's been nominated for twelve and has won five Grammy Awards.

Victor has the kind of musical spirit that doesn't come along every day. Perhaps because of his seemingly inborn talent or his exposure to such high-level players at such a young age, Victor not only has a unique connection to creativity, but he's also able to articulate that connection. He has published two books, 2008's *The Music Lesson: A Spiritual Search for Growth Through Music* and the 2021 sequel, *The Spirit of Music: The Lesson Continues*. Both books capture that elusive relationship between artist and art. They serve as a lesson in how to let the muse in. He puts those lessons into action through regular retreats and courses at his Center for Music and Nature, which is based out of Wooten Woods, a 150-acre camp owned by Victor and his wife, Holly, and is located on the Duck River, west of Nashville, Tennessee.

Given all those pieces, it's not surprising that he has a thing or two to say about chasing—and finding—tone. His first bass was a Univox violin-shaped bass, a copy of Paul McCartney's Höfner. It was the only bass his parents could find that was small enough for him to handle. When he was twelve, a Series 1 Alembic bass showed up in a local music store. Stanley Clarke, well-known for playing Alembics, was a huge influence on Victor, and need-less to say, he fell in love with the instrument. Recognizing the connection, his parents bought it for him. Even though it was too big for him (and still is, according to Victor), the Alembic was his main instrument for the next seven years as he played countless shows and recorded with his brothers.

"We were gigging a lot," says Victor. "Then, during a recording session with my brothers, the producer wanted a different sound. We were in the studio working with a guitarist named Ira Siegel. He said to me and my brother, 'I have some friends that are making basses. Would you like for me to call them?' I thought, 'Sure, why not?'"

Unbeknownst to Victor, Ira's friends were Joey Lauricella and Vinny Fodera. This was 1983, and the two had just opened the doors of Fodera Guitars—at the time, a small shop in Brooklyn, New York, with a simple mission: "To build an instrument that would look and sound phenomenal; an instrument that you just can't put down."

"Joey Lauricella showed up at the studio with two basses," Victor contin-ues. "I fell in love with both of them. When I put my hands on that Fodera bass, it just felt like me. That's the best way I can explain it. I don't even think I plugged it in. It just started with the feel of that bass."

Victor did end up choosing between the two, and in an incredible act of generosity, Joey told Victor to keep the bass and send him the money when he had it. Victor explains,

> Nobody does that, especially to an unknown kid. Maybe it was because our record deal was supposed to be a big one, and he knew he was going to get the money. But anyway, from that day on, I just fell in love with that bass.

The only way for me to describe the sound is that it was me. It just sounded like me, and that has been the sound I've been recreating all the time. Now that I have a little name for myself, I've gotten some basses made, but every time I do it, it's based off that sound.

Victor's bass was a Fodera Monarch, serial no. 037, with an EMG PJ pickup set (precision-style in the neck position, jazz-style in the bridge slot). Victor shares,

In 1983 I didn't know anything about pickups. I just played the bass. I just knew how to play music. And I knew that this one felt and sounded good. The next bass I got was another Fodera, and it had EMG pickups in it too. That's when I really started learning about that first bass's PJ style. My second bass had J pickups. It was still a Fodera Monarch, same model, but a different style. It still had my sound but slightly different. It was then that I started paying attention to pickups. Now the only time I don't want that sound is when I might be working for someone who wants somebody else's sound. They might want my style but a different sound. But when I want to just be me and my voice, it's EMG pickups with the P and J style.

One of the challenges in this tone-chasing game is articulating, defining, and putting into words just what constitutes one's sound. There's no common language. One person's *dark* is another one's *deep*. *Bright* can be chiming or tight. With a philosopher's mind, Victor can dig deep and identify the unidentifiable: his sound.

"I could put it this way," he continues.

If you think about a drum set—not a drum but a drum set—a drum set sounds complete. There are lows, highs, and everything else in the middle. If you just tried to support a band with a snare drum, you could do it, but it wouldn't be the same as having a bass drum too. Now you've got the bass drum and the snare drum, you might need some toms in between that. You might need a cymbal to shine on the top. Then it feels complete.

Well, my bass playing is the same way. And even though I have many bass heroes, I really patterned myself after Stanley Clarke. He could play the best bottom end bass for Chick [Corea] or for whoever he's playing for. But he can cut through on the top with this rapid-fire, snare drum-type stuff that just cuts. I grew up in that era, my sound was patterned after him, and the EMG pickups do that perfectly. I didn't really realize that at the time, in 1983, that that's what it was. But now that I've been able to use a lot of different pickups with different sounds, I realized, for me, it's the EMG pickups that give me that full, what I'm going to say, the "drum set sound."

If I just need to get on the bottom of the music, like what bass players do, I can just play the bottom end, and it's fat. If I want to do a little feel away from the bass range and get into the midrange of the instrument, it's clear. But then if I want to go Larry Graham-style and start thumping on the bass, there need to be lows and highs because I need the snaps and the pops to cut through. Not all pickups are designed to do that. Some just do what the bass is designed to do, be all fat on the bottom. But the EMGs gave me the full range of lows, mids, and highs. And when I play fast, which I do a lot, and rhythmic, which I do a lot, the pickups can take it.

For Victor, the instant he held that Fodera bass in his hands, there was a connection. In 1983 Victor was on the verge of transitioning from a child prodigy in his brothers' band to an undeniable musical force in his own right. Here, once again, is a situation where the company's and the player's evolution mirror and feed off of each other. Fodera was in its infancy when Wooten became one of their first players. Their relationship is still tight today. They're family. In 1983 Rob and EMG were a few steps ahead of Vinny and Joey, in terms of their business, but Rob's connection with Victor was strong, too, and continues today for many of the same reasons.

Victor explains the following:

As I started to get a little notoriety, I started being able to speak to companies directly and get some endorsements and things like that. I learned pretty quickly that I am endorsing people, not just a company. So I started early forming relationships with people. The company may grab my attention, but what's going to keep my attention is the people I'm dealing with. I look at it like a marriage. She might be beautiful, but now I've got to meet her parents. I need to meet the family. I mean, you know, that's the only way it's going to work. I can't go off beauty alone. I can't just go off "These pickups sound great. Let me endorse them." No, I need to like who the people behind the pickup are.

Who is EMG? What do they stand for? That's the start, but then they need to like me too. That's the way a marriage works. That's the way a relationship or a friendship works. That's the way a musician and an instrument works. I may love the sound of it, but if it doesn't feel good to me, if it's not responding to me, I can't play that bass.

Back in the late eighties, early nineties, I started to be able to form relationships because the Flecktones were becoming popular. I made relationships with people that I liked. And Rob has been one, for me, since the beginning. I guess you call it an endorsement. He was one of my early ones because, by the time the Flecktones hit, I had been playing that Fodera bass and those pickups a good seven years or so. I was deeply rooted in that sound. Rob has been there for me and a lot of other people from the very beginning—my very beginning, anyway.

Some reach the goal early. Some search a lifetime and never quite get there. In 1983 Victor may have been only nineteen, but he'd been playing professionally for fourteen years already—an amazing blend of innocence and experience. In one sense, it's fair to say that he found his sound (or maybe his sound found him) early, and he's been running with it ever since. But that doesn't capture the story.

In true Victor Wooten fashion, he best sums up the game like this:

I have my sound and I know what it is. But I tried other things. And if I hadn't tried that other thing that day back in '83, I wouldn't have found my real sound. Growth is about exploring, experimenting, succeeding, failing. So I urge people out there to continue to explore.

My hat is off to Rob and everyone at EMG for doing what they do and for having done it for so long at such a high level.

9

THE JOURNEY
CONTINUES

Rob Turner: It's been a busy couple of weeks. I'm working on a couple of really intense projects, and I'm struggling.

Jim Reilly: What's causing you grief?

RT: Well, we have this Jim Root model. It's one of the Retro Actives, and we're not sealing the coils. We've been doing them for a while, and we don't wax the coils or anything. I'm just not real happy with that. We haven't had any complaints, which is fine, and because it's an open-coil pickup, it's not that big a deal. But we're not waxing it. The thing is, when you wax it, it ruins the entire finish on the top of the coils. And then when you put a logo on it, it looks even worse. It just doesn't work.

So we made this ultrasonic bonder to bond the top of the bobbin.

The coil is wound, and then we skim off the top of the bobbin. Then we put this piece on what we've molded, called the snap cover, and we ultrasonically bond it, or at least that's what we've been trying to do.

The problem is that there's wax on the bottom of the bobbin that has to be cleaned off. So we're working on creating this heater that heats up the wax and then spins the bobbin. You know, like one of those things you used to have when you were a kid, and you made a painting with one of those things where the paper spun around? It's the same sort of thing but sitting horizontally instead of flat.

We've also been playing with creating this sort of hot-air knife. It produces hot air and melts the wax on the bobbin. And then you spin the pickup in that hot air, and it takes the wax off the bobbin. It sounds simple.

JR: *Actually, it sounds really complicated.*

RT: *It is. It's way more complicated than it should be.*

JR: *The obvious question then—if nobody is complaining about the pickups not being waxed, why are you waxing them?*

RT: *Because we need to make a product that is solid when it goes out the door. I don't want somebody coming back. I don't want Fender coming back, going, "Hey, we've got five hundred of these things, and we've gotten a complaint from one customer. What are you going to do about it?"*

When you wax them, the air space around the pickup is confined, and you know that the coils are solid. You get a more consistent result rather than when somebody sort of squeezes the bobbin and wraps it with tape and hopes that the air is sort of trapped.

Anyway, it's become a bit of a fiasco, but I've learned a lot, and I'm having a good time. It's helped our automation procedures. I'm working with Tom Nelson, and he's into it too, so . . .

Perhaps more than anything else, the conversation above gives the most revealing glimpse into Rob's work. Sonically, there were no issues with the Jim Root pickup. From a construction and quality standpoint, all was fine. There were no problems. No one complained, and maybe no one ever would. But a little issue picked away at Rob, and he needed to find a solution. He could have left it alone and moved on, but that's not Rob.

The easiest way to get to EMG world headquarters is to fly into the Charles M. Schultz–Sonoma County Airport, near Santa Rosa, California. From there it's less than a mile to 675 Aviation Boulevard and EMG's factory, warehouse, and corporate offices. You could walk there in about fifteen minutes.

Flying into San Francisco International Airport and driving up through Mill Valley, San Rafael, Petaluma, and Santa Rosa is a much nicer route. Along the way, you pass close to Metallica's headquarters in San Rafael and then a little further up the road, the old Grateful Dead headquarters. Other musical landmarks dot the scenery, including, a little closer to EMG, the

MESA/Boogie amplifier company. Driving directly would only take about an hour and a half. Add another half hour of driving time, and only a slight detour will take you through Sonoma and the heart of California wine country. Regardless of whether you're a wine connoisseur, the detour is worth it for the scenery alone. For the wine/prog rock enthusiasts, Les Claypool's Pachyderm Station, the home of Claypool Cellars winery, is a must stop.

Regardless of how you arrive, you'll find an interesting dichotomy. While some envision a rock-and-roll mecca with rock stars hanging around the front door, in reality, EMG is a pretty unassuming-looking space in an industrial park that looks pretty much like any other industrial park. Inside, there are EMG artist pictures on the walls and testing areas with guitars and basses, but beyond that, it's just a factory making a product—unassuming in almost all regards.

What sets EMG apart—and has done so since the beginning—are the people working in that facility. While EMG artists immediately recognize that they are a part of a family, that's nothing compared to those who work there.

When general manager Gary Rush retired, Andy Gravelle took over the company's day-to-day business management. Gravelle came from Jetronics, another Santa Rosa company specializing in custom cable assemblies, magnetics assemblies, subassembly components, and other electronic parts. In his new role as EMG's chief operating officer, Andy decided to take the temperature of the employees' morale and get to know them a little bit. One by one, he called people into his office and asked, "Who do you work for?" He expected to hear EMG or their immediate supervisor. To a person, everyone answered, "Rob."

Rob's commitment and connection with those who work for him is reflected in their loyalty and the connection they feel in return.

"We've had many employees working with us for years and years," Rob says. "Silvia Lopez, who works in coil winding, Mahadev Desai, there's a family group named Jacinto—mother, aunts, uncles, cousins—have all worked with us. Then there's Miguel and Sandra Hernandez, Imelda Tapia, and maybe a half-dozen others who have been with us for over thirty years."

The music business is artist driven. If this story has shown nothing else, it's shown how critical the artist's role is to a music-product business's success. Along with the Turner brothers, Gary Rush, and Hap Kuffner, many others have played key roles in getting EMGs into artists' hands. A small handful of those are noted below.

In recent years the job of connecting artists to their tone through EMG has fallen to Tommy Armstrong-Leavitt. "I got my first set of EMGs in a guitar that I bought in the parking lot of the music store where I was teaching," he says. "This guy had a guitar he was trying to sell because he needed to make his truck payment. The store didn't want to buy it, so I followed him out to the parking lot and bought it myself. I got this hot-rodded, custom-built guitar that had two 85s and an SA. That probably was in 1987. I was fresh out of music school and was in a pretty popular band. That was my first set of EMGs, and I just found my home with those pickups."

Tommy's official connection with EMG began about ten years later. He was making a record with his band, Hurt, with longtime EMG artist Devin Townsend producing. Townsend insisted that they use one specific guitar, with EMG pickups, for all the tracks.

"It was an ESP Explorer that he claimed was sent to James Hetfield," says Tommy. "Devin said that James didn't like it, so they sent it to him, and he wouldn't send it back."

At the time, Tommy was playing several different guitars, but only a few were equipped with EMGs. Seeing the value in outfitting all Hurt's arsenal, Townsend offered to introduce Tommy to Jack Nau, who, at the time, was handling EMG's artist relations and North American sales.

"This was back when you sent your press kit in the mail," Tommy continues.

I sent my big, fancy envelope with all the stuff and waited. I called a few times and finally got him on the phone a couple weeks later. I said, "Hey, Jack, this is Tommy from the band Devin Townsend told you about." I'm sure he was thinking, "Crap, not this guy." But he said, "Listen, kid, I heard your record. I don't much care for your style of music, but I'm sure somebody likes it. Here's how it works. Here's the honest truth. If you want to use EMG pickups, we can help you out and give you half price as an artist's accommodation." Before I could say, "Great! Thank you!" he continued. "You know, even Zakk Wylde pays for his pickups. Nobody gets a pickup for free." That was the beginning of my professional relationship with the company."

That professional relationship grew steadily over the years to the point where EMG was sponsoring Tommy's instructional clinics and supporting him both as a player and an educator. In 2014 when they were looking for someone to pick up the artist relations work, they called Tommy.

"I was a headbanging, professional musician and educator my entire life," he says, "literally, from the time I was eighteen. Technically, the job at EMG is my first real job. When they called, I was playing in five bands, teaching full-time. I knew the guys in the sales department, and they said they were looking for a new A&R guy. The next thing I knew, I was taking a tour and moving up to Santa Rosa."

The circle was complete—Tommy went from the kid who played the gear, to an artist getting a deal, to a mainstay performer on the company's roster, to the guy whose job it became to take care of both the young kids like he had been and the A-listers who represent the product.

"Funny story," he continues. "We were emptying out some old filing cabinets, and I found a letter from Metallica typed out on their letterhead inquiring about endorsement opportunities. I also found handwritten receipts signed by Sharon Osbourne for buying pickups for Zakk Wylde. That confirmed it. Everybody bought their pickups. Of course, as Zakk became more and more popular, he got a better and better deal, and now it's to the point where we actually send checks to Zakk."

Before Tommy, Chrys Johnson handled artist relations. He manned that post for almost three years before taking on a similar job with guitar string, pick, and accessory giant Dunlop Manufacturing. The first real dedicated North American sales manager was Doug Marhoffer. With Hap handling overseas sales, Doug's focus was on taking care of the markets closer to home. According to Doug, though, "National Sales Manager" may have been how the business card read, but in truth, he covered all the bases— artist relations, marketing, and product development, along with overseeing North American sales.

Marhoffer joined the team near the end of 1991. He was working for Washburn guitars in Chicago, but when the band he was playing in broke up and with the prospects of another Chicago winter looming, he decided he needed a change of scenery. Initially, he reached out to his friend Jol Dantzig at Hamer Guitars. Dantzig didn't have anything for him but knew that Rob was looking and suggested that Marhoffer give EMG a call.

"So I called Rob," Marhoffer continues.

We had a chat, and it went well. The next step was for me to talk with Hap. Hap and I hit it off right away. A couple of weeks later, I flew out to Santa Rosa for an interview with Rob and Gary Rush. Two weeks after that, I was packing up all my stuff in a U-Haul trailer and moving to Santa Rosa.

When I got there, I went in for my first day of work. Rob handed me my first paycheck and a bunch of brochures with things to do around Santa Rosa and said, "Take the week off and get to know the area." I've never had a job before or since where they gave me a check and told me to go mess around for a week, but that was pretty typical of the way Rob did things.

The guitar world was in the midst of a complete transformation as Marhoffer took his place at EMG. The studio world with guitar-driven rock and racks of effects units was about to be crushed under the weight of grunge. Aggressively pursuing OEM relationships, particularly with ESP guitars, expanding the range of acoustic pickups, and broadening the EMG Select line with Cort's Jack Westheimer kept EMG strong in the marketplace. Marhoffer also spearheaded the prewired Pickguard series—a complete set of artists' signature pickup combinations mounted and wired onto a pickguard that could be dropped into a Strat-style guitar body. The series started with David Gilmour, Kirk Hammett, Steve Lukather, and Vince Gill models and a "YNH" ("Your Name Here") model, which could be customized with the player's pickups of choice. In 1996 Marhoffer served as the connection between the artists and EMG to create the company's 20th Anniversary series, once again featuring special models from Gilmour, Hammett, Gill, and Lukather.

Doug's time with EMG was filled with stories of meeting and working with some of the world's best musicians, opening deliveries and finding guitars like David Gilmour's red Strat, phone calls from the Reverend Billy F. Gibbons, and road trips with Rob and Hap.

Shortly after the 20th Anniversary series, Doug left EMG. He was young, single, and needed a little more excitement than the sleepy towns Northern California could offer. EMG laid the foundation for a music industry career that took Doug to DigiTech and then to Røde Microphones.

The enigmatic Jack Nau filled the vacancy left by Marhoffer's departure. Rob and Jack had crossed paths but weren't much more than passing acquaintances. Jack was a local who had grown up in Sonoma County. He was fairly well-known as a graphic artist and designer. His claim to fame in the graphic arts world was working for the artist Christo. Christo and his partner Jeanne-Claude gained fame and notoriety for their grand, environmental art installations, many involving wrapping natural landmarks in fabric or stretching fabric over long distances. In Northern California, they're most famous for their piece called *Running Fence*, a veiled fabric fence spread out over twenty-four and a half miles in Sonoma and Marin Counties.

"Karen and I were at a wine tasting," says Rob, "and we ran into Jack and his wife. I mentioned that we had lost our sales manager. He basically looked at me and said, 'Okay, I'm your new sales manager.' That was on a Friday night. Monday morning, he shows up at the office, and he goes, 'Yeah, I'm your new sales manager,' and so he just sort of worked his way into the company."

Although very capable, Jack could be a polarizing figure in the music business. While he was instrumental in connecting and strengthening the relationship with the young rock players, like Zakk Wylde, he could be equally alienating to some of those EMG artists who had been around for a while, like Steve Lukather.

It worked from a business standpoint, though, and the company saw huge growth with Jack on board. Jack was an accomplished guitarist who could speak the language with pros and beginners alike. The booths at the trade shows were packed. Jack did a great job bringing in artists for all manner of promotional opportunities. Eventually, though, Rob and Jack didn't see eye to eye on his role in the company. They had other philosophical differences as well, so Jack left the company. Tragically, shortly after leaving EMG, Jack suffered a fatal heart attack while onstage playing with the band of his son, Sebastian.

After Jack, Rob went on the hunt for sales managers and found Scott Wunschel. Prior to EMG, Wunschel managed sales for Nady Wireless Systems. Scott stayed on board until about 2018. With his departure, EMG had no need to look outside the company for a replacement. Rob's daughter, Alison, had been working in the family business since 2013. She had worked her way up by doing odd promotional tasks and through the sales team and business development to the point where she was ready to take on the post of vice president of North American Sales.

While the thread of working in the family business was woven through-out Rob's and Bill's childhood and continued through Matthew's and Alison's, there were differences. EMG headquarters in Santa Rosa was about twenty-five minutes away from the Turner home in Petaluma. There were no capacitor-winding or soldering lessons going on in Rob and Karen's garage. Regardless, the company and the family were (and still are) inseparable. Both Matthew and Alison, along with their cousins (the sons of Rob's sister, Pam) Andrew and Patrick, all worked for EMG. Matthew and Andrew worked in OEM (Original Equipment Manufacturers) and distributor sales. Patrick did graphic design.

Matt joined the company full-time in 2010, but the lines between family and factory had been blurred long before that. There may have been no hollow core door workbenches in the current Turner generation's home (Matt claims there wasn't even a soldering iron), but when Matt was old enough, he spent summers making pickups and doing odd manual labor jobs in the factory. His earliest EMG memories—and where he first realized the scope of his dad's work—were at NAMM shows in Anaheim.

"I would have been around eight when I went to my first show," Matt says. "I absolutely loved it. I pretty much went back every year since then. We would use that as an opportunity to go on family vacations. We would go to Disneyland. My grandparents were down there too. It was like a circuit: Disneyland, NAMM show, visit the grandparents."

Growing up, Matt kept busy with school, sports, and mandatory piano lessons, but nothing really planted deep roots and took hold. After graduating from San Francisco State University in 2010 with a history degree and with the US job market only just starting to recover from the most severe downturn since the Great Depression, Matt jumped at the chance to join EMG.

"There were a lot of things that I wanted to learn at EMG," he continues.

And I wanted to be part of the family business. I figured it would work out for me perfectly. I could have my life in the city. I'd be able to make money. I'd be able to work with my dad.

I learned a lot about the manufacturing process and what goes into it. I have a bit of the tinkerer in me, like my dad. I love building computers, I'm really into that. So I was really interested in what goes into the manufacturing processes. I worked in coil winding. I ran the SMT (Surface Mount Technology) machine.

I didn't do potting, but I worked with the injection molding machines and built pickups. I didn't do everything, but I had a full picture of how everything worked.

The inner workings of the factory were interesting enough, but the real lessons Matt learned came from the relationships between EMG, their customers, and EMG players. His title may have been under sales, but according to Matt, it wasn't *sales* in the traditional sense. By this time, EMG's customer base had long been established. Along with his cousin Andrew, *sales* really meant taking care of OEM clients like ESP and Schecter, who accounted for the vast majority of business at the time, travelling to factories around the world, meeting distributors, and manning the trade show booths.

The travel was definitely the highlight.

I saw some of the most amazing things, traveling for EMG. Going to factories in Asia is insane. I went to the PT Samick factory in Indonesia. It's one of the largest factories in Indonesia. If you're standing in the middle of it, you cannot see either end, it's so big. They make pianos, guitars, any kind of wood-based instruments you can imagine. I met all kinds of representatives from different companies who don't normally go to NAMM shows, sourcing people, consultants, people on the fringe of the music industry but whose work is within it. Also, and this is not related to the business, some of the most amazing meals I've ever had in my entire life have been while when I was travelling for EMG—crazy stuff in Korea, Japan, China, places like that.

Matt only stayed with EMG for a little over five years. While, in many ways, the work was engaging and fulfilling, his passion for guitars and music often paled in comparison to those he was working with. Needing a change and a bit of an adventure, Matt left in February 2016. At the time of this writing, that adventure has landed him in Seville, Spain. The lessons learned at EMG about personalization and taking care of customers has served Matt well in his current job: deployment manager for the online vacation service Glamping Hub. Think Airbnb with unique, exotic accommodations, and you've got Glamping Hub. If you want to stay in a yurt with an ocean view or a tree house in a rainforest, Matt is your guy.

While he's found success outside of EMG, the family business is in his blood, and Matt sees himself returning someday. It's hard to separate the family from the company. That thread has been firmly woven into the Turner family's fabric.

"I'll probably end up going back to EMG at some point," he says.

> It's always going to be a part of my life. I don't really know when that's going to happen. But I feel like because I went off and did my own thing, I gained the confidence and experience that I feel like I could come back at it at some point, add a real value, and be able to do something and feel good about it. We'll see.
>
> As I get older and realize how much my dad was dealing with and how much he has accomplished—he's done some really amazing things, and he's kept it together—I'm just really proud of him.

Alison took a more circuitous route to EMG, but there seemed to be little doubt in her mind that she would end up following in the family's footsteps. "I must have been a senior in high school," she says, "and my brother had just started college. He wasn't really sure what he was going to do. I was going to go to college, but I didn't really know what I wanted to do either. My dad took me out for dinner, just the two of us, and basically said, 'Okay, this is all up to you, but I just want to know, is EMG something you'd be interested in?' 'Of course,' I said. 'Why wouldn't it be?'"

Alison studied business at California State University in Sacramento. After graduating, she took an internship with D'Addario in New York. The lessons learned by working for one of the largest music industry manufacturers in the world proved invaluable when she returned to Petaluma and EMG. Perhaps most important, although she respected and valued the enormity of an operation like D'Addario, what she really wanted was the personal connection and relationships that already existed at EMG.

While Alison was in New York, Scott Wunschel gave her a few East Coast accounts to manage, an opportunity to get her feet wet and test the EMG waters. When she returned to the West Coast, she started in a sales assistant role and gradually added more and more responsibilities to her plate. There really was no question that Alison would move into the top sales job by the time Scott left. By 2021 she was overseeing the international markets as well, had "North American" dropped from her title, and changed her business cards to read, simply, "Vice President of Sales."

Alison has a unique perspective. Not only is she literally connected to the company's lifeblood, but she can also step back and see the business as a whole. Her understanding of what makes EMG work seems to be reflected by many others. First, the engineering and innovation falls on Rob, and his will be tough shoes to fill—not that Rob is planning to retire anytime soon. More than likely, he'll be the guy working, tinkering, and creating till they have to pry the soldering iron out of his hand. Second, EMG is such a well-oiled machine that the work ahead will be to improve efficiencies, streamline production, and refine products, not reinvent the industry.

"Rob has always been great not just at making the product," she continues, "but at making things more efficient, like taking risks on different automation and trying new technologies to make the products cleaner, neater, sharper, and just nicer in general. Those are the things I will be able to carry on since I can't carry on the actual engineering. But you know, we have over seven thousand SKUs (Stock Keeping Units—unique codes for individual products). EMG is not lacking in a product line. Rob has definitely set this thing up for as long as anybody keeps playing electric guitar and bass."

When asked about the factors behind EMG's longevity and success, despite ever-changing trends, fads, and a marketplace, her reply, once again, echoes others: "I would say there are two parts," she elaborates.

It's the product itself. And then I would say it's Rob as a person and how he's been able to manage the company over the years. I think my grandpa was like this in his businesses too. There's just a very natural decision-making process. It's just straightforward and easy. Rob makes these decisions that you kind of think, "Oh yeah, that's obviously the right decision." But I think a lot of people don't necessarily make those choices.

I think that's reflected in how long people have worked for him. When you have a quality product and the person who you're working for genuinely cares that everything coming out of the business and going to the customer is of high quality, sounds good, and looks good, then all the employees take up that cause too. They take a lot of pride in their work. I also really like that our company feels small. It still feels very family owned. I know everyone who works here.

Maybe the final piece is that Rob really has no interest in doing anything that doesn't seem like a natural fit for EMG. He doesn't want to be in the effects pedal business, for example. He would never make an instrument. That's just not for him. When you talk about making amplifiers, he pretty much says, "Hell no, get it away. It's too big. It takes up too much space." I think he sees all these things that other companies take on and says, "Why would you mess with something that works? Why would you? Why wouldn't you just chug along, create new products that fit, and keep doing what you do?" I think, for us, rather than looking outward at what other people are doing, it's more like we ask, "How do we do what we do better? How do we fill the gaps in our marketplace?" I don't really see that changing. EMG can keep going on forever.

The Tom Nelson that Rob talks about at the beginning of this chapter owns Machine 10LLC. The company specializes in machine design, motion-control software, and automation. Tom lives in Petaluma and has done a lot of work designing the automation machines and programs for EMG. Through Rob, Tom has connected with many other music industry folks in the area—notably, MESA/Boogie. When Gibson bought Boogie at the beginning of 2021, they were looking for ways to modernize and streamline production, and they turned to Tom.

As Rob reflects on working with Tom to find solutions for the Jim Root project, he sees his father reflected back. Bill Sr. used to get together with like-minded friends, and almost like a sport, they would dive into problems, imagine solutions, invent gears or sprockets or gizmos to make the navigation system of a model airplane, or pursue some equally engaging pursuit/work.

Rob and Tom's relationship is a professional one. Money changes hands. But more than that, it's the meeting of two like minds who are equally driven to dive into problems, imagine solutions, and invent fixes. Solving the Jim Root pickup-sealing problem took two weeks and found them on a Sunday driving 151.9 miles south to the Harbor Freight store in Los Banos, California, because they sold a plastic heater with a compressed air attachment. The pair needed a way to experiment with a device that could control both the airflow and the temperature simultaneously, and the closest device that could even potentially manage this was that five-hour round-trip away. The next day Rob went over to Tom's, sat down, set up the little plastic heater with compressed air, and started playing. After three mornings spent with Tom, they hit pay dirt and had created a machine to do what they needed it to do. They created a product that in turn created a product.

While Rob sees his father, I see the evolution of a process that defines Rob from the beginning. No doubt he inherited both this natural inquisitiveness and, perhaps more important, the drive to find the solutions through genetics and osmosis from the Turner lineage. But, like all lineages, Rob has taken it further, beyond what anyone could have imagined when he was first inspired by the sixties' rock gods.

While Rob never articulated it this specifically, his father instilled in him the need to have a product that was not only one's own but would also feed inquisitiveness and fuel creative passion. It certainly doesn't hurt that Rob's product lives in the hands of rock stars. The music business has no shortage of intriguing characters, mystique, and charisma. As long as you don't buy into that mystique and charisma too much, simply working with those intriguing characters is rewarding in itself.

Rob went from watching the Grateful Dead and Jefferson Airplane at the Melodyland Theater to working with Bob Weir and Jack Casady, from being inspired by their sound and their innovation to helping them craft and create their sound.

There's a magic between the creator and those who make the tools used to create. Both are artists, equal in their own right. Neither could exist without the other—two forces combining to create the magnificent. Rob says that it's like a race car. The driver isn't going to be the one who builds the vehicle. Rob can play a little bit of guitar, but he's no David Gilmour. But the race car driver and the race car builder must be connected. They must be expressions of the same creative impulse, or no race will be won.

Perhaps that's the heart of the work, that connection to the rush of endorphins when one taps into a creative force. "When I finish a project," Rob says, "when something's off my desk, especially if it's a major undertaking, I'm elated. It's a relief. It's like I can take a deep breath, relax again, go, 'There it is. It's done.' Relief is probably the wrong word. It's more a release. It's a high, a definite high."

In the end the question becomes, "What drives you?"

When asked, Rob takes a deep breath, sighs, becomes introspective, and replies in the following way:

> I mean, it has a lot to do with being in business and being successful. When you've been in business for as long as we have, not every year is a winner. Not every product you make is a home run, by any means. But one thing about the music business is once you turn something out, it becomes yours. You can never give it up—unless you just fall to pieces. Pretty much anything that EMG makes, promotes, and puts out into the marketplace never leaves the catalog. I don't think there's anything that we've actually ever totally stopped

making. Maybe we don't make the seven-string orange version anymore, but there really isn't anything that we won't do.

So there's the business, but it's more than that. Ultimately, I think I've just found a wonderful way to fuel my inquisitiveness, my search. I think that's what it comes down to. And I can choose where I want to go with my search.

There's an unofficial musicians' litmus test when choosing a gig. Before the "Yes," the gig needs measuring based on three factors (not necessarily in the following order): the music, the money, and the hangout. In a perfect world, every time a player steps onstage, the music is rewarding, the money is good, and your bandmates are fun to be around. Of course, if none of those boxes are checked, it's an easy "No." One isn't enough to sustain you for long. If you're only playing for the money, you hate the music, and you don't connect with the other players, the gig may put food on the table, but it won't be long before you're looking for more. It's the same if you love the music, hate the players, and aren't making any cash.

You need a minimum of two out of three. Music you don't really connect with can be overlooked if you're hanging out with good friends, especially if your bank account is full. Similarly, if the money isn't there, projects with great music and good people can be taken on to greater or lesser degrees, depending on one's alternate sources of income.

Looking back on Rob's story and legacy, I see these same evaluative measures at play since the very beginning. Just replace "making music" with "designing sound." He was able to do the uncommon and turned a hangout with his brother and their friends into a product and a business that reaches worldwide. To this day he's balanced the profitable work with the work that engages the soul—a path of least resistance. And always, every single time, those projects and products that stick are the ones that grow out of strong, rewarding personal connections.

There hasn't been a single artist, builder, or craftsman whom I spoke with while putting this project together that hasn't said some form of "being an EMG artist or working with Rob is like being part of a family" or commented on how the engagement and joy Rob exudes when he sinks his teeth into a challenge is both obvious and contagious. While he's traveled a long way from the Turner family hollow-core-door workbench, at his core, Rob is still that kid hanging out in his parents' garage, tearing apart his brother's ES-335.

EPILOGUE

A Note from the Author with Thanks

All the Chapman Stick's electronics are housed in a removable, interchangeable module. I've played the Stick, Emmett Chapman's instrument created for maximizing his unique, two-handed tapping method, for almost thirty years at the time of this writing. So much has come through my connection to the Stick, Emmett, and the Stick community, not the least of which has been my connection to Ned Steinberger, which led to connecting with Rob and this book.

The Stick was also where I first realized the pickup's significance and impact on an instrument's sound. Since the Stick's electronics can be changed so easily (this was before the solderless EMG connectors), one of the first things I did when I started experimenting beyond simply the Stick's technique was to swap my passive Stick pickup module for an active one, which housed two EMG Front Tele pickups. I couldn't believe the difference. To my ear it immediately sounded better. What I've come to learn many years later is that "better" is, of course, subjective. What it sounded was "right," to my ears.

At the time I really didn't understand the difference between passive and active pickups. I knew my new Stick pickup module needed a battery, but that didn't matter. I didn't even really understand the difference between high- and low-impedance signals. None of that mattered. All I knew was that I liked the active pickups. They were alive. I had my voice.

Fast-forward to many years later, and with a solid understanding of passive and active pickups and the pros and cons of each, I'm firmly in the active pickup camp. Long before I started this project, before I had even met Rob, all of my instruments sported EMGs.

This was a different project from any of the others I'd previously been involved with. The seeds were planted at the 2020 NAMM (National Association of Music Merchants) show. The Ned Steinberger book (*Steinberger: A Story of Creativity and Design*) was finished and due to be released in a few months, and I had been invited by Jim D'Addario to go out to dinner with him, Ned, and Rob and Alison Turner. I think I was set up—the ultimate blind date. There was an empty chair beside Rob. I sat down and we started talking. Before the evening was done, I had committed to putting together his story. In truth, I was an easy mark. With the Steinberger book done, I was looking for the next victim, and Rob was already at the top of my list.

Shortly after we began, COVID hit.

At first the musical instrument world feared the worst. With the world shutting down, pretty much everyone figured that it was the end. There were far more pressing concerns than guitars, and the world would turn its attention elsewhere. I remember talking with Rob in the first days of mandatory lockdowns. While he was sure that he'd personally be able to weather the storm, he was seriously concerned for everyone else at EMG, as it was almost certain that COVID would shut down the musical instrument world too.

Nothing could have been further from the truth. While the touring and live music world stopped, recording, learning, and instrument sales went through the roof. The combination of stimulus checks and time on players' hands led to an unprecedented boom in instrument sales. No one could keep up. EMG found themselves weeks, even months, behind being able to fill orders. This was new territory.

As for this book, COVID meant I couldn't travel to EMG until the very end of the project to dig through their archives (thankfully, Zoom and Skype filled much of the void). On the bright side, it also meant that many of the artists were captive, too, and much more easily accessible. Metallica, for example, had created a professional sports league-type bubble around their San Rafael, California, headquarters and had the time to add their voices to the project. I found that to be true for almost all the artists who added their voices and shared their place in Rob's story. While I suspect they would have been just as forthcoming and eager to share, regardless of being forced off the road, it undoubtedly made things easier.

The other consistent thread as I worked through this project was the Fender Jazzmaster. As we started this project, Rob was just beginning to be grabbed by the notion of making an EMG pickup system for the iconic Fender Jazzmaster. Over the course of our many conversations, we'd often turn to the Jazzmaster. The project's progress began to signify Rob's way of doing business and the larger factors that fueled the music instrument industry both in times of COVID and simply in general.

To illustrate the point, here are some excerpts from our conversations. On April 29, 2021, Rob said the following:

> I've started with basically just using a Jazzmaster-style coil and magnet setup. I mean, not really different at all, but there's your starting point. Where we want to go is to present EMG as a Jazzmaster-type product. I suspect they'll be fairly traditional, a Fender-style coil, alnico 5, alnico 2 magnets, that sort of thing. We'll put a bump in the midrange just because the pickup with the guitar itself has this kind of an odd bridge, and that gives the guitar a different timbre altogether.
>
> The other thing about the Jazzmaster is that it was never really that popular a guitar. That makes it a perfect guitar for modernization because it doesn't have the sort of Stradivarius-like attributes that the Stratocaster has or that the Jazz Bass has. It's sort of an orphan. That's one of the reasons I like it.

On January 12, 2022, he added more.

> It's the same thing with the Jazzmaster. I've been working on that thing for a couple of years. But the reason I've been working on it for a couple of years is because of COVID. We can't turn out anything new. There's not really a market for it. I mean, there is, don't get me wrong, but we can't make enough product. We can't get enough supplies to make products. Why should I create something new that we can't get parts for? And so with the Jazzmaster, I have to ask, "Do I really want to do this to all my people out on the floor?" That's a lot of what it comes down to. Do we want to take this to the next level?
>
> Alison, Tommy, and Anthony—everybody in the group—is going, "Oh, wow, we could have some fun with this. We can do something with this." I agree, but it's not like a clock is ticking this time.

As always, there are so many people to thank, without whom this project never would have left the ground. As always, thank you, Emmett Chapman (1936-2021). Emmett trusted me to tell his story, which opened up more doors than I could have possibly imagined. Thanks to Ned Steinberger for sharing his story, for being a part of this one, and for providing feedback on early drafts. Thank you to all the artists, builders, and innovators who shared their Rob and tone-chasing stories with me. Your collective voices tell much more than just Rob's and EMG's stories and give invaluable glimpses into how that creative impulse that so wants to be heard breaks its way into the world. You reflect the best of a music industry that found its feet in the seventies, exploded in the eighties, inspires and innovates today, and will continue bringing joy into the world as long as we keep picking up our guitars and playing.

Thank you to Michael Tan, John Cerullo, and the Rowman & Littlefield team for the ongoing support and hard work with both *Steinberger* and this project.

Many thanks to Tom Mulhern for the editing, encouragement, introspection, and perspective on this project and the music industry's many twists and turns over the years. Thanks as well for the amazing foreword, which captured so many of the book's themes much more eloquently than I could have. I've enjoyed our conversations and look forward to them continuing.

Thanks to my DC & The Struggle bandmates, Darcy and Mudgey, for once again giving me the space to experiment with new gear and different sounds, as well as to Ricky for his feedback and encouraging me along the way in the way that only a drummer can support a bass player.

My lovely Lori, thanks again—as always—for the patience and love as I spent countless hours falling down countless rabbit holes and for inspiring the cover. To Karen, Alison, and Matt, thank you for letting me monopolize Rob's time and for sharing your family stories, as well as your incredible hospitality.

And finally, to Rob, thank you for trusting me with your story. I hope I did it justice.

APPENDIX

EMG Artists to Date

Aaron Fink / BREAKING BENJAMIN

Aaron Ruby / WALLS OF JERICHO

Adam Duce / MACHINE HEAD

Adam Dutkiewicz / KILLSWITCH ENGAGE

Adam Zadel / SOIL

Aden Bubeck / MIRANDA LAMBERT

Adhnan Sulaiman / THE POYNT

Ahmad Hani

Ahrue Luster / ILL NIÑO

Al Glassman / JOB FOR A COWBOY

Alan Wallace / EMINENCE

Alex "CHEVAL" Lejeune / LES KROUTES

Alex Al / MICHAEL JACKSON, ARSENIO HALL SHOW

Alex Lofoco

Alex Webster / CANNIBAL CORPSE, BLOTTED SCIENCE

Alexandra Zerner

Alexi Laiho / CHILDREN OF BODOM

Alexia Rodriguez / EYES SET TO KILL

Alexx Calise

Alvaro Padilla / FUSED BY DEFIANCE

Anders Björler / THE HAUNTED, AT THE GATES

Anders Odden / MAGENTA, SATYRICON, DOCTOR MIDNIGHT & THE MERCY CULT

Andre Lassalle / VRBOG

Andreas Farmakalidis / MARTY FRIEDMAN, SOLO ARTIST / PRODUCER

Andreas Kisser / SEPULTURA

Andres Osorio Toledo

Andrew Craighan / MY DYING BRIDE

Andy Irvine

Andy James / SOLO ARTIST

Andy Martis / MEDIA SOLUTION

Andy Martongelli / ARTHEMIS

Andy Sneap / HELL, SABBAT

Angeline Saris / ZEPPARELLA, NARADA MICHAEL WALDEN BAND

Anissa Rodriguez / EYES SET TO KILL

Anneke van Giersbergen / SOLO ARTIST

Anthony Armstrong / RED

Anthony Caetano

Anthony Joyner / SMOKEY LONESOME, CORRINE CHAPMAN, KATA RHE

Anton Reisenegger / PENTAGRAM CHILE, CRIMINAL, LOCK UP

Archaon / 1349

Arkadius Antonik / SUIDAKRA

Arnold Quezada / DIRTY MACHINE

Arttu Lesonen / LOST SOCIETY

Ashley Purdy / BLACK VEIL BRIDES

Axel "Iron Finger" Ritt / GRAVE DIGGER, DOMAIN

Barney Ribeiro / NERVECELL

Béla Fleck / BÉLA FLECK AND THE FLECKTONES

Ben Carr / MAD SATTA

Ben Moody / WE ARE THE FALLEN

Ben Savage / WHITE CHAPEL

Ben Weinman / DILLINGER ESCAPE PLAN

Ben Wells / BLACK STONE CHERRY

Bill Kelliher / MASTODON

Björn Gelotte / IN FLAMES

Blake Bunzel / IN THIS MOMENT

Blasko / OZZY OSBOURNE

Bob Froese / PRIDE TIGER

Bobby Keller / SOLO

Bobby Thompson / JOB FOR A COWBOY

Bobby Vega

Bobzilla / HELLYEAH, DAMAGEPLAN

Bone Maggot

Brad Lang / FOREIGNER/RATT/ Y&T

Brandon Sigmund / HOSTILITY

Brendon Flynn / FREYA

Brendon Small / DETHKLOK

Brent Hinds / MASTODON

Brent Rambler / AUGUST BURNS RED

Brent Riggs / JOB FOR A COWBOY

Brian "Hardgroove"/ PUBLIC ENEMY

Brian Ashley Jones

Brian Harrah / YETI

Brian Lowe / NOEL HAGGARD, CLINT MOODY

Bruce Hall / REO SPEEDWAGON

Bruno Mars
Bryan Richie / THE SWORD
Bryce VanHoosen / SPELLCASTER
Buz McGrath / UNEARTH
Byron Stroud / 3 INCHES OF BLOOD
CAT / STATE LINE EMPIRE
Celso Rossatto / NEVERNATION/ MARIA ALZIRA
Cesar Soto / MINISTRY
Chad I Ginsburg / CKY
Chad Kroeger / NICKELBACK
Chad Smith / HEMLOCK
Chance Shirley / MITCH GRAY & THE MUSIC MILITIA
Charles Elliott / ABSYMAL DAWN
Charlie Parra del Riego / SOLO ARTIST / DIFONÍA
Charlie Simpson / FIGHTSTAR
Charly Sahona / SOLO ARTIST, VENTURIA
Chelsea Baker / AROARAH
Chris Babbit / TAKING DAWN
Chris Beattie / HATEBREED, BLACKENED
Chris Cannella / AUTUMN´S END
Chris Dawson / SEASONS AFTER
Chris Garza / SUICIDE SILENCE
Chris Howorth / IN THIS MOMENT
Chris Kells / THE AGONIST
Chris Rawson / WALLS OF JERICHO
Chris Robertson / BLACK STONE CHERRY
Chris Rubey / THE DEVIL WEARS PRADA
Chris Storey / ALL SHALL PERISH
Christian Bernadac / ALL MISERY
Christian Lee Vasquez / SECTAS
Christian Olde Wolbers / FEAR FACTORY, ARKAEA
Christopher Hertel
Chuck Goff / TOBY KEITH
City of The Weak
Claude Colmars / DUSK OF DELUSION
Claudio "El Pastor" Filadoro / BUFFALO
Claudio Sanchez / COHEED AND CAMBRIA
Cody Webb / AGES APART
Cole Rolland
Colin Edwin / PORCUPINE TREE, NO-MAN
Colin Goheen / OUR VINYL VOWS
Constantine / DESCENDING, MYSTIC PROPHECY
Corey Barhorst / KYLESA
Corey Feldman / TRUTH MOVEMENT
Corey Krick / ESSENESS PROJECT, BLOOD RED
Craig Martini / PAUL GILBERT
Cristiano "Pizza" Migliore / LACUNA COIL
Curt Chambers / FRANKLIN BRIDGE, P-DIDDY, LL COOL J
Daisy De La Hoya

Dale Stewart / SEETHER

Damon Marks

Dan Jacobs / ATREYU

Dan Kenny / SUICIDE SILENCE

Dan Veall

Dane Markanson / GLASS CLOUD

Daniel "DL" Laskiewicz / THE
ACACIA STRAIN

Daniel Bonfogo /
CLAUSTROFOBIA

Daniel Freyberg / CHILDREN OF
BODOM

Danielle Evans / AUTOMB

Danny Marino / THE AGONIST

Darrell Roberts / SINTANIC

Dave Kushner / VELVET
REVOLVER

Dave Starr / WILDESTARR

Dave Young / DEVIN
TOWNSEND PROJECT

David Briseño / ALL MISERY

David Ellefson / MEGADETH

David Gilmour / PINK FLOYD

David Karns

David Maldonado

David Pearl / STATE LINE
EMPIRE

David Sanchez / HAVOK

David Shankle / DAVID SHANKLE
GROUP

David Tilghman Jr / WESLEY
BELMONT

Dean Back / THEORY OF A
DEADMAN

Decrepit Birth / DECREPIT BIRTH

Derek Tailer / OVERKILL

Diamond Rowe / TETRARCH

Diego Lessa / SALÁRIO MÍNIMO
/ TREZZY

Diego Farias / VOLUMES

Dink Cook / TOBY KEITH

Dino Vidovich / SAGES

DJ Temple / WITHOUT MERCY

Doc Coyle / GOD FORBID

Doug Weiand / SOLO ARTIST

Doug Wimbish / LIVING
COLOUR

Douglas Prado /
CLAUSTROFOBIA

Drew Ofthe Drew / DREW AND JP,
HELICOPRIA

Drew Watterson / ELE

Drew Zaragoza / SINICLE

Driver Williams / ERIC CHURCH
BAND

Dylan Thomas / LANDMINE
MARATHON

Edmond Gilmore

Edsel Dope / DOPE

EKTOMORF

El / AUTUMN'S END

Eli Santana / HOLY GRAIL

Enrico Galetta

Eric Calderone / EROCK

Eric Peterson / TESTAMENT

Erik Leonhardt / TANTRIC

Ethan Farmer / CHRISTINA
AGUILERA, NEW KIDS ON
THE BLOCK

Evan Brewer / THE FACELESS

Evan Seinfeld / BIOHAZARD,
THE SPYDERZ

Evander Swaby / MANSUR
BROWN/JAY PRINCE
Faisal Talal / ACRASSICAUDA
Felipe Nothen / LETTERS INTO
ETERNITY/SOLO
Firas Al-Lateef / ACRASSICAUDA
Forrest French / CROOKED X
Franccesca De Struct
Francesco Caponera / SHADOW
THRONE
Francesco Fareri / SOLO ARTIST
Frank "3 Gun" Novinec /
HATEBREED
Frank Bello / ANTHRAX
Frank Gravis
Frédéric Leclercq /
DRAGONFORCE
Freekbass
Gabe Crisp / WHITE CHAPEL
Gabriel Connor / RED DEVIL
VORTEX
Gabriel Guardian / FYER/
IMMORTAL GUARDIAN
Gabrielle Louise / THE
GABRIELLE LOUISE SHOW
Galder / DIMMU BORGIR
Garrett Zablocki / SENSES FAIL,
STEREO STARGAZER
Garry Tallent / BRUCE
SPRINGSTEEN´S E STREET
BAND
Gary Holt / EXODUS / SLAYER
Gary Wendt / THE GHOST
NEXT DOOR
Gav King / FIELDS OF THE
NEPHILIM

Geezer Butler / BLACK
SABBATH, HEAVEN & HELL
Gene Simmons / KISS
George Constantine Kratsas /
MANHATTAN PROJECT/
SOLO ARTIST
George Marinelli / BONNIE
RAITT
German Schauss
Gildas Le Pape / SATYRICON
Gino Bianchi / FALLEN FROM
SKIES
Glenn Tipton / JUDAS PRIEST
Graham Stirrett / PHEAR,
GRAHAM STIRRETT SOLO
Greg Tribbett / MUDVAYNE,
HELLYEAH
Guitar Gabby / TXLIPS
Gus Sinaro / SINARO
Harry Gandler / MASTIC SCUM
Hector Maldonado / TRAIN
Helmuth / BELPHEGOR
Henkka Seppälä / CHILDREN OF
BODOM
Hernán Hernández / LOS TIGRAS
DEL NORTE
Hussein Haddad / SOLO ARTIST
Hutch Hutchinson / Bonnie Raitt
I.C.S. Vortex / DIMMU BORGIR
Ian Hill / JUDAS PRIEST
Ingmar Petersen / BEEHOOVER
Ivan Ivankovic / SOLO /
THOMPSON
Iván Muñoz / SYNLAKROSS
Jack Blades / NIGHT RANGER
Jack Doolan / CYPHER16

Jack Doom / CORRUPT
  ABSOLUTE
Jack Owen / DEICIDE, ADRIFT
Jackie Parry / DIANTHUS
Jacob Maisonneuve / ARCTOS
Jake Pitts / BLACK VEIL BRIDES
Jamareo Artis / BRUNO MARS
James Barnett / CANE HILL
James Beattie / SEASONS AFTER
James Hetfield / METALLICA
James Khazaal / NERVECELL
James Murphy / SOLO ARTIST /
  PRODUCER
Jari Mäenpää / WINTERSUN
Jasmine Cain / JASMINE CAIN
  BAND
Jason Krause / KID ROCK
Jason Netherton / MISERY INDEX
Jason Newsted / VOIVOD,
  METALLICA
Jay Visser / MORBID SAINT
Jay Wud
JB Brubaker / AUGUST BURNS
  RED
Jeanne Sagan / ALL THAT
  REMAINS
Jed Simon / VIMIC, SCAR THE
  MARTYR, STRAPPING
  YOUNG LAD
Jeff Caughron / JESSTA JAMES
Jeff Hanneman / SLAYER
Jeff Kendrick / DEVILDRIVER
Jeff King / REBA MCINTIRE
Jeff Ling / PARKWAY DRIVE
Jeff Loomis / SOLO ARTIST /
  NEVERMORE

Jeff Pogan / SUICIDAL
  TENDENCIES
Jeff Walker / CARCASS
Jeff Worley / JACKYL
Jenni Tarma / KYLIE MINOGUE,
  JUBILEE
Jeremy Creamer / DAATH
Jeremy DePoyster / THE DEVIL
  WEARS PRADA
Jeremy Kohnmann / WHITE
  EMPRESS
Jeremy Norman / ASH ARIA
Jeremy Wagner / LUPARA
Jesse Cooper / CROOKED X
Jesse Ketive / EMMURE
Jesse Saint / THE AUTUMN
  OFFERING
Jesús Parra /
  CONTRACORRIENTE
Jim Reilly / DC & THE
  STRUGGLE
Jim Root / SLIPKNOT
Jimena Fosado / SOLO ARTIST
Jinxx / BLACK VEIL BRIDES
Joe "Blower" Garvey / HINDER
Joe Lester / INTRONAUT
Joey Chicago / EGYPT CENTRAL
Joey Edwin / SOLO ARTIST
Joey Jordison / MURDERDOLLS
Joey Roxx / BURN HALO
Joey Vera / ARMORED SAINT/
  FATES WARNING
John "JD" Deservio / BLACK
  LABEL SOCIETY, CYCLE OF
  PAIN
John "Slo" Maggard / UNEARTH

John Baizley / BARONESS
John Browne / MONUMENTS
John Campbell / LAMB OF GOD
John Cummings / MOGWAI
John Ganey / I WRESTLED A
    BEAR ONCE
John Lecompt / WE ARE THE
    FALLEN, MACHINA
John McCarthy / TEARS FALL
    DOWN
John McVie / FLEETWOOD MAC
John Outcalt / GOD FORBID
John Paul Jones / LED ZEPPELIN,
    THEM CROOKED
    VULTURES
Johnny Thrash / Bound By Years
Jon Bakker / KAMPFAR
Jon Bodan / HALCYON WAY
Jon Donais / SHADOWS FALL
Jon Lawhon / BLACK STONE
    CHERRY
Jon Maggard / Fist Fight
Jon Miller / DEVILDRIVER
Jon Mulvey
Jon Reshard / VIGILANT
Jona Weinhofen / I KILLED THE
    PROM QUEEN
Jonas Renkse / BLOODBATH,
    KATATONIA
Jonathan Montoya / SALIVA
Jonathan Nunez / TORCHE
Jonny Santos / SILENT CIVILIAN
Jordan Ferreira / ELIXIR ON
    MUTE
Jordan Ziff / RATT/MARTY
    FRIEDMAN/SOLO

Jorge Carmona / VERAX CHILE/
    CIUDAD ZERO
Jose Ferro / THE SCREAMIN´
    LORDS
José Macario / ARCADIA LIBRE
Joseph Vilane / QUEEN
    DEMENTIA
Josh McDowell / CROOKED X
Josh Middleton / SYLOSIS
Josh Palomar / INFINITE DEATH
Josh Paul / DAUGHTRY
Josh Steely / DAUGHTRY
Josh Travis / GLASS
    CLOUD, THE TONY
    DANZA TAPDANCE
    EXTRAVAGANZA
Josh Wilkinson / STONEMAN
Justin Emord / LOVE AND A .38
Justin Sane / ANTI-FLAG
Kaoru / DIR EN GREY
Karim K / THEORY OF THIEVES
Keith Gibbs / SASQUATCH
Keith Urban
Kennon Pearson / ELE
Kenny Serane
Kenny Wicker / OF TYRANTS
Kerry King / SLAYER
Kevin Cordero / FUSED BY
    DEFIANCE
Kevin Keith / THE ELECTRONIC
    JAZZENSEMBLE
Kevin Walker / JUSTIN
    TIMBERLAKE, KANYE WEST
Kieran Johnston / PERPETUA
King / SAHG + I
Kiriakos Bouloubasis

Kirk Hammett / METALLICA

Kirk Powers / POINT BLANK

Kirk Windstein / CROWBAR, DOWN, KINGDOM OF SORROW

KK Downing / JUDAS PRIEST

Koichi Fukuda / STATIC-X, DRUGSTORE FANATICS

Kris Norris / STRAIGHT LINE STITCH, THE KRIS NORRIS PROJEKT

Kurt Ballou / CONVERGE

Kyle Rasmussen / VITRIOL

Kyle Sanders / HELLYEAH

Kyle Shutt / THE SWORD

Kyle Sokol / KING OF DENMARK/RUDE SQUAD/SECTIONED/TRACE OF DAY

Larry Boothroyd / VICTIMS FAMILY, TRICLOPS

Larry Carlton

Lars Frederiksen / RANCID/LARS FREDERIKSEN AND THE BASTARDS

Lasse Lammert / KILLFLOOR MECHANIC

Laura Christine / WARFACE, MELDRUM

Laurent Barnard / GALLOWS

Lee Rocker / STRAY CATS

Leigh Foxx / BLONDIE

Lena Abe / MY DYING BRIDE

Leonid Maksimov / LINDA

Les Claypool / PRIMUS

Les Hall / CROSSFADE, 70 VOLT PARADE

Lionel Dean Jarvis / NELLY FURTADO

Lou Reed

Luca Angelici

Lucas Olano

Luis Kalil / KEEPER ALIVE

Luke Jaeger / SLEEP TERROR - ACROPHASE

Luke Kilpatrick / PARKWAY DRIVE

Lydia Gavin / F1RST CLASS CITIZEN

Maddie Rice / "LATE SHOW WITH STEPHEN COLBERT"

Marc Rizzo / SOULFLY, CAVALERA CONSPIRACY, MARC RIZZO BAND

Marc Stewart / FOREVER THE SICKEST KIDS

Marco "Maus" Biazzi / LACUNA COIL

Marco Martell / MALEVOLENT CREATION

Marco Zelati / LACUNA COIL

Marcos Cruiel / P.O.D.

Marcus Bryant / TANK, GINUWINE

Marcus D'Angelo / CLAUSTROFOBIA

Marcus Henderson / GUITAR HERO

Mario Rubio / THE DARK ALLIANCE

Marius Charlemagne / NJ 30

Mark Heylmun / SUICIDE SILENCE

Mark King / HINDER
Mark Kloeppel / MISERY INDEX
Mark Lewis Yepes / SICKPIG
Mark Michell / SCALE THE
SUMMIT
Mark Zavon / KILL DEVIL HILL
Marten Andersson / STARWOOD,
GEORGE LYNCH GROUP,
LIZZY BORDEN
Martino Garattoni / NE
OBLIVISCARIS/ANCIENT
BARDS
Marty Friedman
Marty O'Brien / WE ARE THE
FALLEN
Maru Martinez / PAPER HERO
Masaki Murashita / MURASHITA
Máté Bodor / ALESTORM, ALL
BUT ONE
Matt Bachand / SHADOWS FALL
Matt Coates / SOLO ARTIST
Matt DeVries / CHIMAIRA
Matt Heafy / TRIVIUM
Matt Kean / BRING ME THE
HORIZON
Matt Martinez / LANDMINE
MARATHON
Matt Tuck / BULLET FOR MY
VALENTINE
Matt Walst / MY DARKEST DAYS
Matt Wicklund / GOD FORBID
Maurice Fitzgerald / SOLO +
BRIAN CULBERTSON
Maurycy "Mauser" Stefanowicz /
VADER
Max Zuccarino / FALLEN FROM
SKIES

Melissa Evila / THE B.A. SISTERS
/ SOLO ARTIST
Menderson Madruga
Michael "ROOST" Russi /
ROOST/HURT/VIB
Michael Byers / SEASONS AFTER
Michael Keene / THE FACELESS
Michael Massions / BLACK BOX
WARNING
Michael Paget / BULLET FOR MY
VALENTINE
Michel Oliveira / CODE 3-7,
SEVEN SEALS OF THE
APOCALYPSE, SOLO
ARTIST
Micky Waters / THE ANSWER
Mike Edgerly
Mike Gianelli
Mike Hasty / WALLS OF
JERICHO
Mike Inez / ALICE IN CHAINS
Mike Keneally / MIKE KENEALLY
BAND, DETHKLOK
Mike Kroeger / NICKELBACK
Mike Martin / ALL THAT
REMAINS
Mike Mulholland / EMMURE
Mike Payette / PRIDE TIGER,
BOGUS TOKUS
Mike Rodden / HINDER
Mike Spreitzer / DEVIL DRIVER
Mikey Cross / TAKING DAWN
Mikey Way / MY CHEMICAL
ROMANCE
Mirko Lehtinen / LOST SOCIETY
Mitch Harris / NAPALM DEATH
Morgan Knoster / AROARAH

Mylena Monaco / SINAYA

Nate Lopez / SOLO ARTIST

Neal Tiemann / DEVIL DRIVER

Nergal / BEHEMOTH

Nguyên Lê / SOLO

Nick Bell / THUNDER CITY SHOUT

Nick Eash / WINDS OF PLAGUE

Nick Kariotis / NICK K

Nick Kopan / OUR VINYL VOWS

Nick Orisino / OBLIVIOUS SIGNAL

Nick Pan / LEAVE THE CIRCUS

Nicki Tedesco / FRANTIC GINGER

Nicklas Sonne / DEFECTO

Niclas Engelin / IN FLAMES

Nili Brosh / SOLO / TONY MACALPINE / MICHAEL JACKSON ONE BY CIRQUE DU SOLEIL

Novy / ROAD'S END

Oli Herbert / ALL THAT REMAINS

Oli Pinard / CRYPTOPSY

Orion / BEHEMOTH

Pablo Holman / ENTERTAIN THE BEAST

Pablo Kravicz / RED DEVIL VORTEX

Pancho Tomaselli / WAR, PHILM

Paolo Gregoletto / TRIVIUM

Pat O'Brien / CANNIBAL CORPSE

Patrick Jensen / THE HAUNTED

Paul Allender / CRADLE OF FILTH

Paul De Maio / ENTERTAIN THE BEAST

Paul DiLeo / NENA, BILLY JOEL, ENRIQUE IGLESIAS, FOZZY, ADRENALINE MOB

Paul Jackson Jr. / AMERICAN IDOL BAND

Paul Masvidal / CYNIC

Paul Phillips / PUDDLE OF MUDD, OPERATOR

Paul Wardingham

Pete Rafael

Pete Tross / LEAVE THE CIRCUS

Phil Demmel / MACHINE HEAD

Phil Fasciana / MALEVOLENT CREATION

Phil Sgrosso / WOVENWAR

Piotr "Peter" Wiwczarek / VADER

Prashant Aswani / SOLO ARTIST / PRODUCER

Preston Black / TRIPKASE

Primal Age

Prince

Quintin Berry

Ralph Santolla / OBITUARY

Rami Mustafa / NERVECELL

Randy Cooper / EMPERORS AND ELEPHANTS

Randy Morris / TRUTH MOVEMENT

Ray Suhy / SIX FEET UNDER

Reb Beach / WINGER, WHITESNAKE

Rebecca Scammon / CHAOTIC NEGATION

Réda Boucher / BREAK THESE SHACKLES

Reece Fullwood / EUMERIA / SOLO ARTIST

ReLLiM / BLUE FELIX

Ric Markmann / HEART

Ricardo Quattrucci / OLHO SECO/ DARRUA/ESCOMBRO HC

Rich Eckhardt / TOBY KEITH

Rich Ward / FOZZY

Richard Z / RAMMSTEIN, EMIGRATE

Richie Faulkner / JUDAS PRIEST

Rick Marcel / THE ISLEY BROTHERS, CHARLIE WILSON, LITTLE WAYNE

Rick Savage / DEF LEPPARD

Ricky "Freeze" Smith / MORRIS DAY AND THE TIME

Ricky Garcia / LAFEE

Ricky Phillips / STYX

Rik Fox

Rob Arnold / CHIMAIRA

Rob Barrett / CANNIBAL CORPSE

Rob Cavestany / DEATH ANGEL

Rob Heskin / TRUTH MOVEMENT

Rob Milley / NEURAXIS

Robb Flynn / MACHINE HEAD

Robbie Harrington / RONNIE DUNN

Robbie Merril / GODSMACK

Robert Harper / THE MINISTRY OF RECONCILIATION / CITY CLICK / ADMIRAL STAR

Robert Trujillo / METALLICA

Roberto "RA" Díaz / SUICIDAL TENDENCIES

Roger "Tiny" Kohrs / UNKNOWN HINSON

Ronnie Sanchez / GROOVESESSION

Roope Latvala / CHILDREN OF BODOM

Rose Deocampo / INFINITE DEATH/COWGIRLS FROM HELL

Rusty Cooley / DAY OF RECKONING

Ruyter Suys / NASHVILLE PUSSY, DICK DELICIOUS AND THE TASTY TESTICLES

Ryan Butler / LANDMINE MARATHON

Ryan Cano / I, OMEGA

Ryan Meranda / IXION / ONLY HUMAN

Ryan Peake / NICKELBACK

Ryan Phillips / STORY OF THE YEAR

Sacha Dunable / INTRONAUT

Sacha Lévesque / SESSION MUSICIAN / SOLO ARTIST

Sal Coz Costa / MY DARKEST DAYS

Samy Elbanna / LOST SOCIETY

Sara Beth / KILL SLOWLY

Sarah Longfield / THE FINE CONSTANT

Sarven Manguiat / GROOVESESSION

Scott "Cammo" Camarota / CODY MARKS

Scott Eames / NEVALRA

Scott Hull / PIG DESTROYER
Scott Middleton / CANCER BATS
Sean Hall
Sean Long / WHILE SHE SLEEPS
Sean O'Bryan Smith
Sean Watson / DISPLAY OF
  DECAY
Sean Williamson
Sebastian Barrionuevo /
  AVERNAL
Sebastian Jensen / SUIDAKRA
Sebastian Nau / HILLSIDE FIRE
Sebastian Silva / SILVER TALON
Seidemann / 1349
Sergey Golovin / SOLO ARTIST
Sergio Chotsourian / LOS NATAS
Sergio Vallin / MANÁ
Seth / BEHEMOTH
Shane Blay / OH, SLEEPER
Shane Clark / 3 INCHES OF
  BLOOD
Shaun Glass / THE BLOODLINE/
  REPENTANCE
Sheldon Reynolds / EARTH,
  WIND & FIRE, BRIAN
  CULBERTSON
Sin Quirin / MINISTRY,
  REVOLTING COCKS
Sinan Cem Eroglu
Skuewolf / DIRTY WOLVES
Sparky Voyles / MISERY INDEX
Spyros Lafias / CHRONOSPHERE
Stavros Marinos / BIO-CANCER
Stefano Benfante / SHADOW
  THRONE
Steffen Kummerer / OBSCURA

Steinar "Azarak" Gundersen /
  SATYRICON, SPIRAL
  ARCHITECT
Steph Carter / GALLOWS
Stephen "Thundercat" Bruner /
  SOLO, ERYKAH BADU,
  FLYING LOTUS
Stephen Brewer / WESTFIELD
  MASSACRE
Stephen Carpenter / DEFTONES
Stephen Lally / OF TYRANTS
Stephen McGrath / BILLY IDOL
Steve Favela / BANG TANGO/
  COLOR OF CHAOS
Steve Klein / NEW FOUND
  GLORY
Steve Lukather
Steve Smyth / FORBIDDEN, THE
  ESSENESS PROJECT
Steve Stevens / BILLY IDOL
Steve Stine
Steve Winwood
Steven Bradley / I WRESTLED A
  BEAR ONCE
Stitches / RAVEN BLACK
Stuart "Rage" Dixon / VENOM
Stuart Hamm
Sulene / SOLO ARTIST /
  COMPOSER / HELICOPRIA
Sydney Ellen
Taylor James / HILLSIDE FIRE
T. D. Clark
Ted Aguilar / DEATH ANGEL
Ted Morcaldi / MAD SATTA
Teloch / NIDINGR
The Commander-in-Chief

The Giving Tree Band / THE GIVING TREE BAND
The Mendenhall Experiment
Thom Turner / FREYA
Thrust
Tim Bertsch / JADED MARY
Tim King / SOIL
Timothy Bailey, Jr. / ARIANA GRANDE
Tish Simeral
Tod Howarth / FOUR BY FATE
Tom Araya / SLAYER
Tom Eaton / HAND OF FIRE
Tommy Armstrong / SOULMOTOR / TESLA
Tommy Bolan / NYC - RICHIE RAMONE BAND
Tommy Borboa / TRADITIONS
Tommy Denander
Tommy Stinson / GUNS N´ ROSES, THE REPLACEMENTS
Tony Aziz / ACRASSICAUDA
Tony Campos / STATIC-X, MINISTRY, ASESINO
Tony Lazaro / VITAL REMAINS
Tony MacAlpine / SOLO ARTIST / PRODUCER
Tosin Abasi / ANIMALS AS LEADERS
Traa / P.O.D.
Travis James / HILLSIDE FIRE
Travis Miguel / ATREYU
Travis Sykes / GLASS CLOUD
Trevor Peres / OBITUARY
Tristan Klein / SOLO ARTIST

Troy Sanders / MASTODON
Tyler Contreras / CRANIAL ENGORGEMENT
Vahan Aslanyan / CARTOGRAPHER
Vashon Johnson / MILEY CYRUS BAND
Vernon Reid / LIVING COLOUR
Victor Brandt / SATYRICON
Victor Guilherme Firmino / MATTILHA
Victor Wooten
Vikki Spit / SPIT LIKE THIS
Vince Gill
Vinnie Hornsby / SEVENDUST
Virus / DOPE, DEVICE, LORDS OF ACID, BIG AND RICH
Vivian Campbell / DEF LEPPARD
Wayne Findlay / MICHAEL SCHENKER GROUP, SLAVIOR, NO SKY TODAY
Wayne Lozinak / HATEBREED
Wayne Static / PIGHAMMER, STATIC-X
Wayne Swinny / SALIVA
Wes Fareas / NAME
Wiley Arnett / SACRED REICH
William Seghers / NEURAXIS
Wolf Hoffmann / ACCEPT
Wolfgang Van Halen / VAN HALEN
X-Hail / BLUE FELIX
Xander Demos / CLUB SHRED, INTO THE ARENA
Yvette Young
Zac Tiessen / SOLO ARTIST

Zach Broderick / NONPOINT
Zach Myers / SHINEDOWN
Zach Wilson / CHOICES

Zakk Wylde / BLACK LABEL
  SOCIETY
Zoltan Valter / SECTIONED /
  JALATH

INDEX

ABOUT THE AUTHOR

Chasing Tone continues **Jim Reilly**'s exploration into the relationship be-tween musical instrument designers and those inspired by their creations. An accomplished musician in his own right with degrees in music, jour-nalism, and education, Reilly has both a unique point of view and a deep understanding of music and musical instruments. His ability to connect with players, builders, and those driving the music business translates into insightful and engaging stories. From his home in Calgary, Alberta, Canada, in addition to writing feature-length books, Reilly has contributed to many music industry magazines, helped other musicians and artists share their stories, and has had his work featured on CBC Radio One. For more infor-mation, please see www.jimreilly.ca.

Scan for the *Chasing Tone* Spotify Playlist featuring many of the artists, music, and instruments featured in this book.

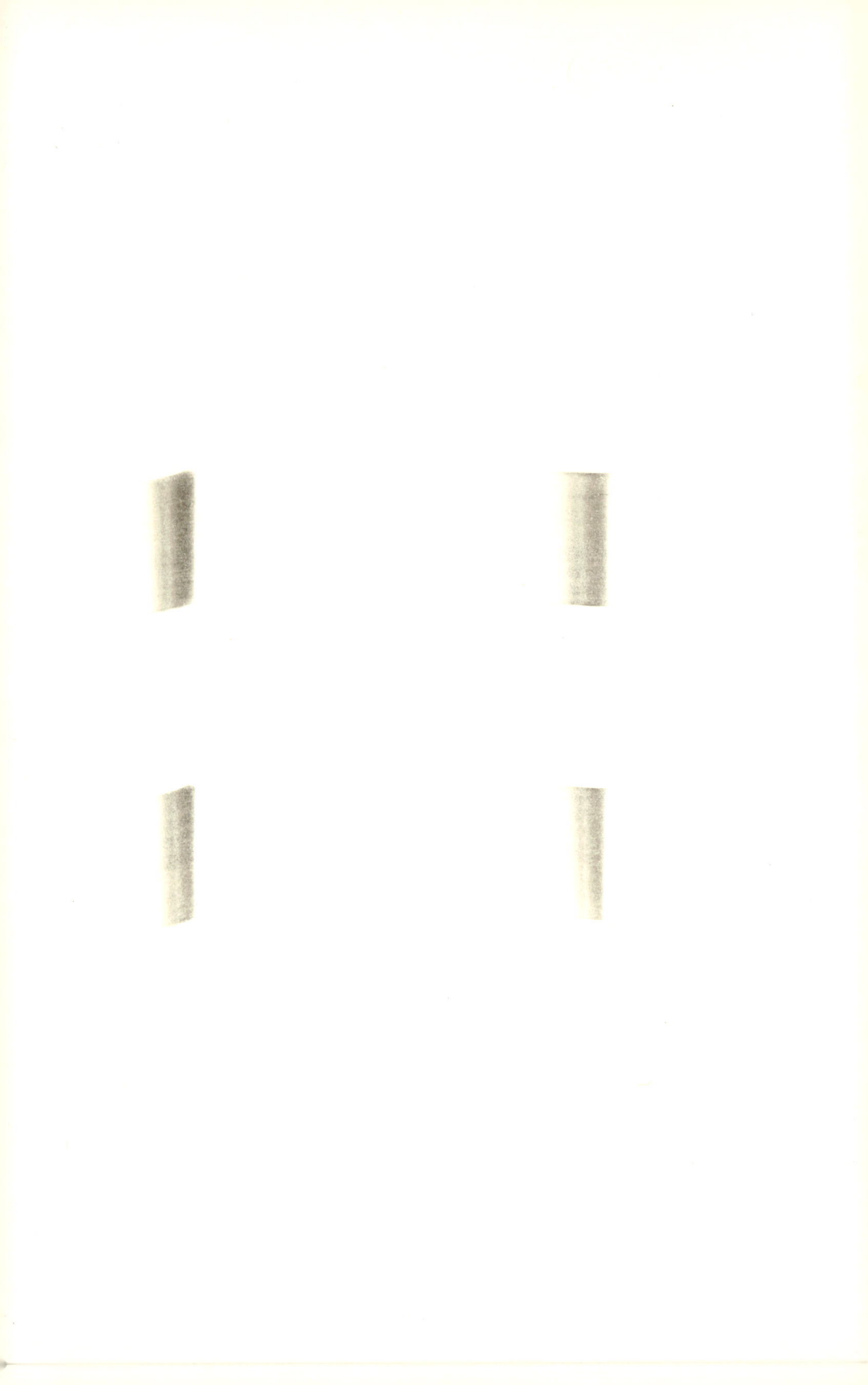